CHRISTINE McGUINNESS

A Beautiful Nightmare

CHRISTINE McGUINNESS

A Beautiful Nightmare

mB

MIRROR BOOKS

This book is dedicated to my children.
Leo, Penelope and Felicity, you are the
reason I live, love and laugh every day.
You all make me so proud, I am
incredibly blessed to be your mummy.
I love you to the moon and stars
and back.

MIRROR BOOKS

1

Published in Great Britain and Ireland in 2021 by
Mirror Books, a Reach PLC business,
5 St Paul's Square, Liverpool, L3 9SJ.

www.mirrorbooks.co.uk
@TheMirrorBooks

Hardback ISBN: 9781913406714
eBook ISBN: 9781913406721

Photographic acknowledgements:
James Rudland, Christine McGuinness

Design and production by Mirror Books.

Printed and bound by CPI Group (UK) Ltd,
Croydon, CR0 4YY.

Contents

Prologue: Being Myself 1

1. Humble Beginnings 7

2. Overcoming 21

3. We Are Family 37

4. Pageant Life 49

5. Nobody Puts Christine In The Corner 53

6. Troubled Twenties 63

7. Becoming Mrs McGuinness 77

8. Our Little Twinkles 85

9. Three Is The Magic Number 105

10. Meet My Beautiful Children.................................... 117

11. Mammoth Milestones 133

12. Dealing With Diagnosis 147

13. A Day In The Life 159

14. Back To School 163

15. If You've Got Laughter, You've Got Everything.... 175

16. All That Glitters 187

17. Christine McGuinness, Celebrity? 197

18. Making A Difference 213

19. Confidence.. 231

20. Chameleon 243

21. Over To You 267

Prologue: Being Myself

I don't know why I'm here. Patrick wanted me to come with him, but I really don't feel confident and my dress doesn't look quite right. I don't think I've eaten today. Oh God, I hope no one speaks to me. Who's that? I recognise them. Maybe if I smile and keep walking, they won't stop and talk.

Oh, Patrick's chatting to someone, everyone speaks to him, they haven't acknowledged me. That's fine, I've got nothing to say anyway. Why am I here? I should have stayed at home. God, I hope people aren't going to watch me eat. Ah, there's our table. Where's my seat? I can't see the Christine place card anywhere. I can see Paddy McGuinness and there's… 'Paddy's wife'. Great…

That was my internal monologue at an event I attended a few years ago with my husband Patrick.

It's quite a regular thing to be referred to as 'Paddy's wife' and to barely be given a second glance when we're out together.

I'm used to it, and I love being married to my husband.

I'm proud to be his wife. But I am Christine and I want people to know about my life – before and after I took my husband's surname.

That doesn't mean to say I'm not apprehensive about you reading this memoir. There is so much that has happened and an abundance of trauma I've been through that no one knows about.

Not because I've ever tried to hide anything. Whenever I've been interviewed, whether that be for a press call for The Real Housewives Of Cheshire or on a red carpet at a big celebrity bash, no one's ever asked me a question about myself.

I've never been quizzed about my childhood, or my teenage years, or why no one even knew my name for a decade while I was married to one of the biggest presenters on TV.

Every interview was about him. *What does he think? What's he really like?* So, it's high time I had my say.

Don't get me wrong, I'm not fame-hungry and I'm not even sure I even want to be considered as a 'celebrity'.

But behind every decision I make, every time you see me on TV and every job I accept, there's one crucial reason behind it – my children!

As many of you know, Patrick and I are parents to three incredible kiddies – twins Leo and Penelope, eight, and our five-year-old daughter Felicity.

Very early on in their little lives they were all diagnosed

with a life-long condition, autism. As heartbreaking as it was at the time to find out, and our worries for their future still exist, I'm trying to make a better world for my babies.

Everything I do, including writing this autobiography, is to raise vital awareness for this hidden disability that is so unrecognised in our society.

And I hope by the time you've reached the end of this book, you will have a better insight into what being autistic means – from the biggest challenges we face to the greatest joys and achievements we get to celebrate.

There's been such huge movements in diversity over the last couple of years, and I'm determined to follow suit and change the stigma around autism.

According to the National Autistic Society, there are 700,000 autistic adults and children in the UK, which equates to one per cent of the population.

While there are an estimated 3 million family members and carers of autistic people in the UK. These statistics are huge and I'm hellbent on raising awareness whenever I can.

Every move I make in this crazy industry that is showbiz is inspired by my children.

There is so much that isn't widely publicised or known about autism, and it's my pleasure to share my experiences as a parent to my three amazing children. Even if my story helps one person, then I've done my job.

But make no mistake, and the title gives it away, there are going to be things in this book that will be hard to read.

There are so many tough moments that I've been through, situations I've found myself in and things that have happened to me that can only be described as horrendous. But as the name of my book also suggests, I've tried to take something beautiful from each of these nightmares. Because I believe that even in times of trauma you can gain strength.

I've not held back, there will be revelations that will shock people. But I'm doing all of this for the children and to raise awareness for autism.

This really is no-holds-barred. When I first agreed to share my rags to riches tale, I decided I was only going to do it if I could write it openly and honestly, and that's what I've done. I really do believe you'll know me quite well by the time you've read the final page.

And I feel more ready than ever to tell my story, because I feel in a really good place in my life.

From birth to the age of 30, things just happened to me and I had no control over anything. But since hitting the fourth decade of my beautiful nightmare, I've actively lived life as best I can and I really feel like this year is my best so far.

I'm a mum to three children I adore, I'm in a happy marriage, my career is reaching new heights and I feel more capable than I ever have done. I am Christine McGuinness: campaigner, 'TV personality' and now author.

But I was born Christine Leahy – on March 20, 1988, in Blackpool.

When I was a teenager, my mum changed my surname so that myself and my two siblings all had the same. I became Christine Martin.

And on that note, let me take you right back to where my beautiful nightmare started...

1

Humble Beginnings

I've only ever stolen one thing in my life.

When I was a child, I attempted to take a pair of shoes from the local Asda. My school shoes had holes in them and I was getting bullied about it.

Much to my horror, I got caught and the police came and took me in a back room to give me a telling off. They also called my mum in.

The shop assistant spotted my battered loafers.

"I'm getting bullied and I've got holes in my shoes," I wailed to this complete stranger.

"I can't afford new ones for her," my mum said, mortified. And seeing how little we had, they let me keep them.

My childhood was a difficult one – no two ways about it. Financially, we had nothing and grew up in quite a large council estate in an area called Halewood in Merseyside. We lived in a flat in a high-rise building and there were bars on our windows.

My mum Joanne and I laugh now and say my siblings and I were dragged up. But I wouldn't change it – if you haven't got anything, you don't miss it.

Things became hard financially when my mother left my father, when I was a toddler. She had to separate from him, she had no choice.

Originally, I was born in Blackpool. Mum got a cleaning job there as a teenager, and that's where she met my dad. My father, Johnny, is from a big family too, with Romany gypsy heritage.

Mum had my sister Billie-Jo first at 18, then me at 19. At first, life seemed great. She was madly in love with my dad and at the time he had a good job as an engineer. That happiness wasn't to last forever, I'm afraid. When I was around one, Mum found out my dad was a heroin addict. Mum was such a good teenager – she didn't drink, didn't smoke and never touched drugs. She was very similar to me and just wanted to get married and have kids. Over time, she noticed Dad wasn't quite being himself. He was going out more and more and started acting differently, losing a lot of weight and not going to work. Mum knew something was up.

My dad went down the wrong path and was dabbling in Class-A drugs when he was quite young. I don't think he realised himself that he was an addict. My mum longed for the relationship to work, but when I crawled over one of his needles as a toddler, she knew it was over.

It broke her heart. She was engaged to the love of her life, they had two baby girls and she had to leave him and move back to Liverpool.

After that, I didn't really have much of a relationship with my father. My sister and I never saw him as young children and as I got older, we'd visit him once a year in Blackpool. Dad would take us down the promenade and make us laugh, and I thought it was the best thing ever. Despite his crippling drug abuse, he's always kept his personality over the years.

I wasn't aware that he was a drug addict until a trip to Asda, when I was eight.

A man, I still have no clue who he was, approached me and said, "You're Johnny's daughter, aren't you?"

"Yeah," I replied.

"Oh, your dad's a druggy," he told me, matter of fact.

And that was the first time I'd heard about it. I didn't understand what he meant. *Does he sell drugs?* I thought. *What does he mean?*

As a teenager, I struggled with his addiction and lack of interest in my life. I blamed myself.

My mind kept replaying the same thing. *Was it my fault? Was having two children too much for him to cope with?*

Blame then turned to anger that my dad wasn't there

for us. Times were hard at home and mum was working as much as she could, just to be able to afford to have the heating on and put food on the table. Then, when I started to think about having my own children, my dad's lack of interest in my life really bothered me. Even more so when I actually became a mum. I kept thinking about how he chose drugs over his own kids.

But as I've gotten older, I've realised it wasn't as simple a choice for him. Addiction is an illness and I don't believe he'll ever get better. His parents, my grandparents, tried to get him the best help they could and they paid for him to go to all the best rehabs. They even bought him a little flat and my aunties treated him to furniture to try to help him out. But his addiction would always take over, and every time he'd waste his money on heroin and sell everything anyone had ever bought him.

Unfortunately, that is his life as a drug addict.

He's still the same now. He's one of the longest living heroin addicts registered in the country and he's prolific around Blackpool. I honestly don't know how he's kept going. He's been in and out of hospital so many times. On lots of occasions, the doctors have called us up and said, "We don't think he's going to make it. This is it now."

"Oh my God, he looks like a skeleton. He looks like he's going to die!" I'll say after making a mad dash to the hospital. And then he'll walk out, strong as an ox.

He's had so many abscesses and gaping holes in his legs,

that the doctors have said to us, "We're going to have to amputate." But he's like a cat with nine lives. He gets up and gets on with it and has done for his 30-plus years as an addict.

"I'm going to get off this shit now," he'd say after every bad episode or near-death experience. But you'd just roll your eyes at him.

It's a shame because he's missed out on so much — birthdays, Christmases — even my wedding day. I'd asked him to walk me down the aisle and he agreed. Then came the morning of my wedding and just as I was putting on my dress, I got a call from my auntie who told me he wasn't coming.

Although my dad and I weren't close, I wanted him to be there. It was gutting and made worse by the fact I had to walk down the aisle on my own. That's a day I'll never get back. But maybe that's how it was supposed to be. He didn't raise me, he wasn't in my life, so maybe he shouldn't have given me away.

The thing is, my dad letting me down is nothing new. Countless times as a child I'd go to Blackpool to see him and he wouldn't leave his bed to spend time with me or Billie-Jo. I'd stay at my nan and grandad's house, who lived over the road from my dad — I think they purposely bought that house so they could keep an eye on him. While I was visiting, I'd often find my nan crying in the kitchen, and I never understood why.

"Nan, why are you upset?" I'd ask her.

"Oh, your daddy's still sleeping and you've come to see him," she'd say.

Now I realise she must have been thinking, *your children are here, Johnny, come and see your kids!*

Dad's been in and out of prison throughout my life. He'd always come out looking a lot better and you'd think, *wow, he's put a bit of weight on, he must be clean*. But within days Dad would be back on the drugs.

I remember a time when we thought he was going to die and we went to see him in hospital.

He looked straight at me and said, "Christine, if I die, I'm going to die happy. I've had a good life. I enjoy what I do. I like it. It feels good."

That was so heart-wrenching to hear. But when he said he was happy with what he was doing, I shouldn't be surprised. Over the years, and especially as a teenager, I saw my dad inject heroin into himself, and smoke it.

But I've got no hate towards him, and if it's taught me one thing in life it's to never have anything to do with drugs.

My dad and I are on good terms now, and don't get me wrong, I love him dearly. But I don't respect him. He's missed out on so much – parents' evenings, first dates – all the things you want your dad there for. And what really upsets me is that he's lost out on having a relationship with my family, too.

My husband hasn't met him and our children haven't

either. Both of Patrick's parents have passed away, so the children only have my mum as a grandparent. I must admit, in the past, I've felt guilty that my dad's still around but has nothing to do with us. It's a real shame, because he could have lived a brilliant life. He should have been the best grandad and dad on earth, but the drugs won over his flesh and blood every time.

At the moment, the kids don't really understand that they have a grandad who they've never met, and they've never asked us where Mummy's dad is. But it's the way it has to be.

As much as I feel OK with my dad, and I accept him for who he is, I'm not comfortable with the thought of introducing my innocent children to a heroin addict. That's what he is, how he looks and what he does. I never know what his behaviour is going to be like, either. Sometimes he's fine and other times he can be quite erratic.

He knows all of this and we've spoken about it, but it's still a massive loss for him and my children. They won't get the chance to meet him or have a relationship with their grandad.

Despite all of the hardships a life without a father around has added to my life, I'm so grateful my mum did leave him all those years ago, and that she got Billie-Jo and I away from that situation. She absolutely did the right thing in ending things, as difficult as it was.

A few years after their break-up, he went on to have

another daughter called Bryn. We really thought and hoped it would change him for the better. Sadly it didn't, and his drug abuse carried on.

After leaving my dad, Mum had to start again and raise two baby girls. She moved back to Liverpool and had my brother Jamie with another man. I'm sorry to say that relationship didn't work out either.

After two failed relationships, Mum struggled a lot and battled with depression, which is understandable considering the amount of heartache she'd been through. Financially, things were tough too, but she tried her best. She worked so hard and juggled a lot of different cleaning jobs just to be able to get food on the table.

I remember when it was coming up to Christmases and birthdays, she'd be exhausting herself working so that she could afford to buy us presents. It was difficult for her. She always tried her best, but she had her own demons to deal with as well. We had nothing in materialistic terms. My siblings and I would fight over who could sit in front of the fire during the cold winter months. I got used to hearing my mum crying throughout the night and seeing her wipe away tears.

She was just unlucky with the two men she fell for and sadly, she's never settled down since. Growing up, it felt like Mum permanently had a lot on her plate.

But despite all we went through, life seemed a lot simpler then. We made fun out of nothing. You'd play frisbee and hide and seek. Every neighbour was your babysitter and everyone looked out for each other. Council estates get a bad name, but there is a big sense of community there that you don't get when you live somewhere like where I live now, in Cheshire. It makes you a bit tougher. But it was difficult as a young girl, and I never really had much. At school I really struggled, too.

One of my biggest problems throughout my childhood was my eating disorder. I had anorexia for years and if I'm being completely honest, it still can be a problem in my life now, but I'm getting better. Although I don't think it's something you ever fully get over.

It started when I was around eight, and it was pretty bad for about ten years.

As a child, it was never about body image. Where I'd grown up on a council estate, I knew nothing about celebrities, and I'd never heard of a 'TV star'. There were no models or reality stars around me, and I never thought I was overweight as a child.

I was just very fussy with food – very much like my children are now. I never liked anything with too much colour, texture or smell, and I started skipping meals at school.

I always felt like I didn't fit in, so in the classroom it was OK. But when you went to the dining hall, that was a social experience I just couldn't deal with. Even queuing up for the food used to give me major anxiety. I didn't know where to sit or who to sit with.

Having to socialise and the fear of rejection was a massive thing.

I always eat my food really slowly and so there was that added worry of, *oh God, everyone's going to get up and go and I'm still going to be here because I haven't finished*. I didn't like eating in front of people and I didn't actually like the food itself. There were times at home when we went without food, so I was lucky to have it, but I just didn't like eating.

One of the dinner ladies noticed and asked why I was throwing my lunch away every day.

"Oh, it's just too wet," I told her.

So, in a bid to help me, every single dinner time this lady would make me my own sandwich. It was on dry bread, with one slice of cheese, and she'd cut the crusts off for me. It was my ideal little sandwich.

Even then, I was still overcome with fear of the social side of things. I remember walking around the dining hall once I had my sandwich, thinking, *where can I sit? Who can I sit with?* It looked like everyone was having a great time, laughing, and there I was not knowing where to go or sit.

I hated the whole experience of eating food as a child. I was quite an anxious young girl. Every single day we were late to school, and I'd spend an hour circling around the cloakroom before I'd go into the class – I was so scared of walking into the classroom, late again. But I made myself even later by doing that. I'd overthink everything.

When I went to high school, things got even worse. I'd

come from a small junior to a big comprehensive with lots of pupils, and that's when my eating disorder really got out of control.

The added freedom played a part, too. I was allowed to do what I wanted. I could go home at dinner time if I liked, bring a packed lunch to school, or have a paid-for meal.

I would tell Mum I was eating at school and then told the teachers I was going home. I could totally get away with not having lunch and it was a completely normal thing for me to not eat all day.

I wouldn't have breakfast before I'd leave the house and I wouldn't have lunch while I was at school.

Then in the evening, I would lie to my mum and say, "Oh, I ate at a friend's house." It just spiralled from there.

I was very underweight, and as I got older, body image added an extra layer to my anorexia.

I started getting attention from boys, which was all new and lovely, because I'd never had friends and I was quite a loner. When the boys at school started flirting with me, I certainly didn't want to change the way I looked.

I remember one of the lads commented on my small frame.

"Oh my God, your waist is so tiny," he pointed out, in such a positive way.

In my mind I thought, *oh, he thinks I look nice*. That's where the image part really came into it.

At 14, I remember the other girls at school were talking

about periods and I still hadn't started mine at that point. My mum knew and she took me to a doctor who told her, "There's still plenty of time for her to start." But he warned, "This is down to an eating disorder."

The doctor said I needed to see a dietician and a nutritionist. But even when it came to those appointments, I just worked my way out of it. I became a professional liar and made excuses.

"I rang the nutritionist and she couldn't fit me in," I'd tell my mum.

Any reason not to go. When I did eventually see a professional, I'd just sit there, glazed over.

They just talked away at me, but they weren't physically doing anything. With any kind of eating disorder, or addiction, you don't get better until you want to. And I didn't want to.

Then, when I started modelling, people would go, "Oh my God, you're so slim! You look amazing."

So, then I was thinking, *well, I can't start eating now, everyone thinks I look great.*

I remember going for a casting as a teenager and they told me if I really wanted to make it as a model then I needed to lose more weight. I was already a size 6, and at 5ft 10in I was skin and bone.

It was completely irresponsible for them to say that to me. I'd like to think that it doesn't happen in today's world, but in the brutal modelling industry, it probably does.

So, I went away and dropped more weight. It backfired as I lost jobs that I was booked for, because my boobs shrunk, too. Although I was always very skinny, I was also quite busty. But once my boobs disappeared, the lingerie modelling job I had in the pipeline went with them.

My struggle to eat has stayed with me throughout my life, and when I'm stressed now, eating is the last thing on my mind.

Worryingly, it became a regular thing for me to faint. I fainted all throughout my teenage years and my twenties. My husband has called an ambulance out for me a few times. Even during lockdown, I fainted and had to explain to the paramedics that I just hadn't eaten for a while.

The real wake-up call was when I collapsed when I was alone with the twins. It's something I'll never forgive myself for. Penelope and Leo were in their cribs and I must have leant over to put one of them down. I remember falling down to the ground. I don't know how long I was out for, but it was probably minutes before I came back around. I knew what had happened, as it wasn't uncommon to pass out, but this time was worse because it was the first time it happened while I was on my own with the children.

It solidified in my mind that I just couldn't ever let that happen again. It upsets me just thinking about it, and I'm ashamed of it. I've got to make sure I stay healthy for the kids; I can't risk being unwell. I need to live forever and be around for as long as possible for the children. It wasn't anything to do with body image at that time, I was just stressed. I had two new babies and I struggled to find time to eat. I was really underweight and unhealthy. Luckily, that's never happened since.

Now, I have to consciously remind myself to eat, for the children. As much as I may not want to sometimes, because I'm too stressed, I'd like to think I'd never go back to being poorly again.

The beautiful side I can take from my anorexia nightmare is that it's made me so aware of my own children's food struggles. I have regular conversations with their teachers, because I need to know whether they're eating. It comes from my personal experience of struggling to eat for so long and nobody really noticing. I'd never want that to happen with my kids. One of the symptoms of their autism is strong food aversions. I have them myself and there's no way I'd eat something orange, red or wet, so I understand my children.

I hope the worst is behind me, I certainly don't avoid food anymore. But as anyone with any kind of mental illness knows, it's always lurking in the background, waiting to rear its ugly head. But my anorexia was just one of many struggles I faced as a child.

2

Overcoming

"Why do you have insomnia?" I often get asked.

"Why don't you drink alcohol?" others question.

Like for a lot of people who have lifelong conditions, my constant battle to get more than an hour's shut-eye comes from my turbulent childhood full of trauma. And my reason for a life of sobriety is due in part to my upbringing and situations I found myself in as a teenager.

To say I had a rough ride during my adolescence is an understatement.

As you can probably sense, my lack of confidence posed huge problems for me as a young girl. I struggled with the transition from junior to high school and I ended up being quite badly bullied by a popular gang of my peers.

It was hard because I didn't have any friends to support

me, and the struggle to fit in has been a constant theme in my life.

Throughout infant and junior school I was fine, as I had a friend that I stuck with. Her name was Carla. I remember being so amazed by her because she had a proper mum and dad, and a proper house. To me as a child, I thought they were millionaires! Now, I recognise they were just a normal family.

When we went to high school, there were notable differences there between Carla and I – she was always more outgoing than me.

But she was a really lovely girl. She had a lovely mum and dad, and they'd invite me over to their house and to go for meals.

One day, when I was playing at her house, she had a really bad epileptic fit. Carla and I were singing and dancing in her kitchen when she had the fit, and immediately I shouted for her mum. She rushed in and told me to ring an ambulance while she put Carla in the recovery position.

The ambulance dashed to Carla's house to take her to hospital and I remember holding her hand the whole way there. I didn't understand what epilepsy was and we were probably only eight or nine at the time. She was OK, but they changed her medicine as a result. I actually received an award in junior school for helping her through that. Every year they gave out a citizenship award, and to my surprise they chose me to receive a trophy and tickets to the Liverpool at home football game for saving Carla. It was the first time I was in the local newspaper, the *Liverpool Echo.*

She was a really sweet girl, but we did just drift apart as can happen when you're young. I believe she still lives in Halewood.

Her parents, Marge and Charlie, were quite a big part of my childhood. They looked after me a lot and showed me what a proper family with a mum and dad that both worked was like. Carla was their world, but I always felt like a hindrance.

I think they picked up that there were some difficulties going on at home, and I overheard them talking one night. It was a conversation I shouldn't have heard, but me being a curious kid I was earwigging. I think they just knew that things weren't great at school and at home for me, and they were discussing whether they should tell anyone about it. Not really understanding, I always questioned, *am I in the way? Am I naughty? Am I a problem?* But thinking back now, they were probably glad I was there with Carla and we had a nice little friendship.

When I moved to high school, it felt like there were thousands of people there that I didn't know. I really struggled.

The other pupils I was with at junior school were all placed in different classes, and Carla eventually made other friends. So, right from the off, I was quite a loner.

I couldn't blend in with the musical group or the drama or sporty cliques, as much as I would have liked to. And my eating struggles added another dimension to my isolation.

I missed out on socialising, because dinner time was the only period when you could sit and have a laugh with your friends. I didn't have one meal throughout high school, so I definitely didn't mix with others then.

And the bullying was bad. It started when I was around 12 and I didn't have friends who were girls.

Looking back, it was when the boys at school started showing an interest in me that the bullying and name-calling reached its peak. I always got on better with boys. I was so innocent and not very streetwise, like my kids are now, and didn't really understand flirting, or why boys were giving me attention.

I never considered it might have been because they fancied me. I didn't think I was pretty, and I had no confidence or friends. I was just glad to have someone speak to me, it didn't bother me that it was from a boy.

The popular girls in class didn't concur, sadly. They really didn't like that the boys were showing an interest in me and that I had a laugh with them.

The male friendships I'd made weren't a conscious choice. I would've loved to have had loads of girl friends, but I just didn't seem to fit in anywhere. I struggled with socialising and I wasn't that confident. I wanted to be liked, but I just wasn't.

Overcoming

I got my first boyfriend, Michael, when I was 12. I still think to this day he's one of the most handsome men I've ever seen in my life. All the girls fancied him at school, and I couldn't work out why he was interested in me. Our mums knew each other and we were in the same year group.

He used to come over to my house and we walked to school together. It was really innocent and the furthest we took our relationship was a kiss. It was quite sweet actually. My first ever kiss was with Michael, and it was on Bonfire Night. Just as we were puckering up, the sky lit up with fireworks in the background. It was magical.

But I got bullied for having a boyfriend. I was branded a slag, which was ironic because I'd never done anything sexual in my life. And it was a bit hypocritical, because there were other girls talking about having sex and going on the pill.

I never wanted to say, "I've actually never kissed anyone," because others had and I wasn't sure what was normal.

It was a summer fling, but because having a boyfriend made the bullying worse, I split up with him. I had a lucky escape really, as I've since found out he went to prison.

When I started getting into modelling, that spurred my tormentors on further.

The pageant world came about for me because of Mum. She could see I was struggling and didn't have any friends, so she wanted to get me out and about. I was pleased. I always wanted to do dance or drama, but you had to pay for those classes and we could never afford it. I was obsessed with the film Dirty Dancing and just really wanted to do something.

My mum had seen a competition in the local newspaper for a beauty contest. It was free to enter, so she signed me up straight away. Much to my surprise I won the competition; it was Miss Junior Merseyside and for taking the crown I was awarded a modelling contract.

I started working on some good jobs around Liverpool, and I was on the billboards in the city centre. It was so good for me, because it got me out of the house. And most importantly, I met new people!

Although in true beautiful nightmare fashion, I got bullied for my modelling success at school.

"Who do you think you are?!" the girls would shout at me.

"Do you think you're someone now? You're not Miss Merseyside – I am!"

When I think about it now, it was really silly and childish stuff, but at the time I was absolutely gutted. The sad thing is, I would have done anything for those girls to be my friends. And it was awful because I was frightened of going to school. I used to speak to the school counsellor quite a lot and tell her I didn't want to be there, but nothing was ever done about it.

I quickly became accustomed to hibernating at home and bunking off. Mum lost it one day.

"Why don't you just go out?" she said.

"You're a teenager, you shouldn't be sat in. You should be out doing stuff."

She probably didn't have partying and drinking in mind when she said that, but she wanted me to enjoy my life and gain some confidence.

So I did. I went out with some of the boys who had shown me attention, some older guys, which was just the wrong crowd, but I wanted to fit in. It didn't go to plan and I ended up going down the wrong path.

When I was actually at school, I was being sent to detention all the time, getting told off and not doing my work. I really struggled with lessons anyway. I could never stay focused in the classroom and academically everything felt like a challenge.

My attendance was terrible – at one point, it was below 20 per cent, because I was always truanting.

I didn't like the social side, the food, just being there, being told what to do, the work, the pressure and I detested speaking out loud. Oh, you could not pay me £20million to go back to school – I hated it.

Mum was fuming and there were constant arguments. I'm sorry I put her through that, and one of my biggest regrets is upsetting her. But I was struggling. I had no support at school or real friends, my mum was suffering with depression and I was battling anorexia.

And the absence of my father played on my mind, too.

When I went down that bad path, I started thinking, *God, I wish I had a dad*. I really hated him for what he'd done and that he'd chosen drugs over us.

I felt like I didn't really have anyone.

I'm not surprised Mum was so angry with me, because my drinking as a teenager got out of control.

These days, I am completely sober. People always ask why I haven't touched a drop in years. There isn't really one reason, it's just a culmination of bad experiences that made me realise I'm better off without it.

Of course, my dad's addiction issues (he was also an alcoholic as well as a drug addict) played a huge part. I became aware at a young age how alcohol and substances can decimate your life.

And of course, my booze binges as a teenager put me in some dangerous situations.

Not many people know this, but when I was 13, I was raped.

It happened at a house party, and as usual I'd been drinking a lot. Anyway, I took myself upstairs in a drunken stupor and got into bed. Not long after climbing under the covers while intoxicated, a boy from school came in and had sex with me, against my will. I remember saying 'no' and I tried to push him off, but I was so drunk I couldn't physically move him.

After that I blamed myself massively. I know as an adult it wasn't my fault, but I still think if I wasn't drunk it wouldn't have happened. But I'm OK, thank God. It's why I'm really protective of my children, the girls especially.

I try to take strength out of any kind of trauma. But there was no denying it was awful. My virginity was taken, and I didn't get to have that special moment with my childhood sweetheart.

I think he was a stupid boy who took advantage. But even to this day, before writing about it in my book, I've only confided in a few people about the events of that night.

I told Billie-Jo and Jamie as an adult and, of course, my husband. And a few years later, I told some friends.

At the time, though, I only reported it to two crucial people – my teacher and my school counsellor.

My history with my counsellor hadn't been great, and she failed to recognise my eating disorder. It took a lot of courage, but I sat down with her one day and told her what had happened on that horrific night.

Instead of a lot of support and advice, which you'd expect when you tell someone in a position of authority you've just been raped, she simply said I must have got it wrong. To my shock, she was more concerned with where I got the alcohol from and why I was at a house party. There was very little sympathy.

In fact, all my teachers and support staff cared about was why I wasn't in my lessons.

There was no help or advice; support that I so needed, and the reason I skived off school so much in the first place. My teachers always told me I'd amount to nothing. I wouldn't get a job and would be signing on the dole. I wasn't an angel at school, so I don't blame them for thinking like that, but it wasn't very encouraging.

They never told my mum about the assault, which is disgraceful.

This all happened 20 years ago, which is crazy to me, because I can remember it so clearly. I'd like to think if it happened to someone nowadays, and they told an adult, something would be done about it. But schools are so busy and overpopulated; how can every single child possibly be looked after?

I plucked up the courage to tell them and they didn't do anything about it. I wonder how many girls that might have happened to.

Every day I thank God I'm OK and I've got the life I have. I'm thankful that I'm away from it and my children are in a good school. I have to trust their teachers to look after them, keep an eye on what they're eating and make sure they're not being bullied.

I speak to all three of them regularly and check that they're happy. I let them know I'm here if there's ever anything they want to talk to me about. The way I am with my children is what I craved as a child. I do believe you become the person you once needed. I'm the woman that I wanted in my life.

And as harrowing as it is for me to open up old wounds,

Overcoming

I'm deeply sad to tell you that being raped at 13 wasn't the first time I was sexually assaulted.

From age nine to 13, I was sexually abused by someone close to our family. At the time, I didn't realise it was abuse. He'd make me watch a lot of videos with sexual stuff in it, and he'd also force me to watch tapes of people being murdered. I didn't understand it or get it.

He'd always talk about sex and masturbating and would take me to his house to make me watch these disturbing videos. I never understood what he got out of forcing me to view this extreme violence.

He'd also take me on days out to places like the beach, and after playing in the sea he would tell me he didn't have any dry clothes. I would then have to travel home naked. If we went to a day out at a swimming pool, he would come into the changing rooms with me. Now I know that's because he was a paedophile.

I never thought to say anything to anyone at the time, because I didn't understand or get it.

Everybody loved this person, and what adds insult to injury was he was investigated for being a paedophile, but he wasn't prosecuted for it.

Everyone refused to believe it at the time and insisted, "There's no way." I actually heard he later went to prison for abusing a child.

My mum was depressed and struggling with her own issues when I was going through the abuse and had no idea this was going on, but a few years later I told her everything. It was heartbreaking for her to find out.

And it's with great sorrow I must admit that the abuse I suffered as a child does affect my life as an adult.

As I mentioned, my sleeping pattern these days is worse than dreadful at the best of times. It takes me ages to drift off and I wake after every hour, or couple of hours. And I believe that's because of the videos he showed me. Not so much the sexual ones, but the films of people being hung. I can't unsee it and most nights I have nightmares. It's absolutely awful. People ask me why I don't sleep, and it's because the bad dreams are so vivid. I don't want to say, "It's because I was abused." I try to deal with it in my own way.

After the rape, sexual abuse and lack of support from a lot of the adults in my life, I just had to carry on going to school and getting on with things.

I continued drinking, partly to block out the sexual abuse and the other trauma I was digesting, but mainly because I wanted friends and I wanted to be social. That was the thing to do. In my later teens, I spent more time drunk than sober. I really enjoyed being completely pissed. I wasn't happy with being just a bit tipsy.

A lot of times I necked a bottle of vodka before I'd even left the house. Like most of my issues in life, I don't think anyone noticed, and I hid it quite well. A night out quickly turned into a four-day bender, and it wasn't until I started my dancing career at 18, which I'll tell you more about later, that I completely knocked drinking on the head.

I wanted control over my life and to make money, and really it was the dancing that saved me.

I hope I've taken something beautiful from my sexual abuse nightmare. As a result, I'm so aware with my own children and I'm very protective of myself.

I realised I was so vulnerable as a young girl. Now, as an adult, if I went out and got drunk, anyone could steal my bag, phone or card. And when you're intoxicated, you're not really in a position to fight the attackers off.

I haven't had a drink since my teen years, not even on my wedding day, and I don't miss it.

I'm not saying I'll never have alcohol again, maybe I will on my 40th birthday. But right now, it's not something that fits in with my life. And I learnt my lessons about the dangers of alcohol early on.

As much as I didn't consciously go, "That's it, I'm never drinking again," I knew I had to stop. Part of me is a little bit worried about consuming alcohol in the future, because I might really love it. I've got quite an addictive personality, and when I really enjoy something that's bad for me, it's just best that I don't do it.

I also knew I wanted to have a family, and I wasn't going to do that while I was drunk – I never wanted to repeat the cycle of what I went through as a child. I really wanted to keep my family together and for my children to have a mummy and a daddy at home, because I didn't have that. And I never want my children to see their parents drunk.

I went through so much at such a young age, and people always ask me if I've had therapy. I never have, although I probably should because of my nightmares. It is something I'm contemplating, but I'm wary. And that's probably because of that dreadful school counsellor. I told her about things going on at home, my parents, that I was raped and that I didn't feel like I had any help or support, and I basically got told I needed to be in my lesson and to go back to class.

That was my only experience with a counsellor – getting the door slammed in my face. It's quite bad when I think back at the lack of support. In terms of my children, the world is moving forward and they're never going to have a childhood like I did, thank God!

In my adult life, I've just coped with everything and I do it quite well. I hope I do, anyway. I've found a passion for the gym and, as cheesy as it sounds, I've found myself. When you've been through trauma, you find joy in anything. You can get down and depressed, which I've been through, believe me. But I just live by the mentality that you've got one life, you've got to live it!

There might have been difficult times, but life's not over and it's what you make of it. You've got to get up and go out and make things happen yourself. You've got to keep smiling and get on with it.

Overcoming

I find life is better when I'm just cracking on with things, rather than focusing on negative stuff or going over it. For me, if I've got a spare hour, rather than sit and talk about negative events from the past that I've put to bed, I'd prefer to spend an hour in the gym, or go for a drive, or have lunch with a friend. I want to live for now and not then.

I think counselling and therapy is great for anyone who feels they need it. But for me, I like to move on from anything negative and live a very positive life. There's something quite powerful about feeling like nothing worse can happen to me.

There's nothing that can happen in my life that is more traumatic than what I've already dealt with.

3

We Are Family

I've never really had a super close relationship with my siblings. Billie-Jo and I have never been really pally with each other, but she and Jamie have the closest relationship.

Growing up I was the middle child, so I think I've got middle-child syndrome. Whereas my sister got to stay up later, because she was the eldest, and my brother got the extra chocolate, because he was the baby, I've always been kind of caught in the middle. It's mad because we all grew up in the same house and probably should have been really close, but we just weren't.

I was very much a loner at school and at home, whereas my brother and sister had big groups of friends.

We're on good terms and we love each other, but we don't see each other much now because of the distance.

My sister's travelled a lot over the years, mainly because her former husband works on an oil rig, but when she's here I'll meet up with her. Jamie and his partner still live in Liverpool. My siblings don't get a chance to see the children often, because we're all so busy. We'll meet a few times a year perhaps, but it's lovely when they do see each other. Other than my mum, they're the only people my children recognise as family.

Billie-Jo has a son and a daughter, my niece Charlotte and nephew Jono, and it's really interesting because although they barely see each other, when the kids do all get together the bond is amazing. My children don't play with any other kids the way they play with my niece and nephew. Their cousins are a little bit older and they seem to get them and they're really patient with them.

My niece and nephew have been raised really open-minded and are aware of autism. We keep saying we're going to see each other more and we should, because the children have such a special relationship.

It's mad because even though Billie-Jo and I are sisters, we never really spoke about things that happened throughout our childhoods.

And when we did actually go on holiday together in our later teens it was a chance for us both to open up.

I'm surprised we even went on that trip, because we weren't close at all. We went to Greece for a week and had a good time and a laugh. We spoke about some things that had happened in our lives and that we never realised about each other until we were adults.

Although I spent a lot of my teenage years either drunk or reclusive, I did have a couple of holidays.

My first getaway was with my partying friend and fellow model Nikki. We used to go out around Liverpool drinking together and although we're no longer in touch I remember her as such a fun-loving, full-of-life girl.

So, at the age of 16, to add to our run of booze-filled nights out, we thought we'd book a little holiday. We didn't have much money at the time for anything too fancy, but we found a two-week package deal to Faliraki for the tiny price of £200. Although the hotel was as basic as you like and left a lot to be desired, it's still one of the best holidays I've ever had.

While on the coach, which was transferring us from Rhodes airport to the hotel, we met a group of Scouse lads who were 16 and 17.

There were six of them and they were amazing and looked after us the whole time. They were such good lads and I look back now and think, *God, what would we have done without them?* They invited us out for breakfast and food, and when we went out to the bars, they'd keep in touch. It was brilliant, because God knows what could have happened to two girls on their own on holiday. It could have been quite dangerous.

In hindsight, we were probably silly going to Faliraki at

16, but it was a fabulous, carefree time. Nothing mattered. We drank fish bowls and partied all night long and I've still got loads of photos from that trip.

I even had a holiday romance with one of the Scousers called Mark, who I met on that coach, and he was just funny.

All throughout my life I've always gone for the comedian. None of my partners have had anything in common looks-wise, but they've all made me laugh. Mark and I never stayed in touch after we flew back home, we both knew it was just a cheeky little holiday romance, but he was a real gentleman throughout. He carried my suitcase up to my hotel for me — there were no lifts in this place. Thinking about it, it was probably the worst hotel in Faliraki, but that's what we could afford, so that's where we stayed. It was just a place to dump our stuff and catch a couple of hours' sleep at the end of the day. And I wouldn't change it. I made such fabulous memories and we were gutted to fly back home.

A year later, when I was 17 and Billie-Jo was 19, she had just met her husband and we decided to jet off on our last holiday before she settled down.

Again, we booked to go to Greece, and again, it cost £200 and was a two-star hotel, but we had a lovely time.

As well as opening up about things we went through as children we just had such a laugh! It's funny, we had so little money and we lived off spaghetti hoops on toast the whole trip, but we were young and free and didn't care. Our purses soon emptied and when we started getting down to our last euros we questioned what to do.

In a twist of fate, we were dancing in a bar one night and a lady came over and said, "Can I speak to you?"

I had my hot pants on with a little lacey top and I was really going for it on the dancefloor. I used to feel so much more confident back then when I was showing a bit of flesh. Anyway, we followed this lady into the back office and she handed us 40 euros each.

"Will you dance on the bar?" she asked.

Immediately we said yes. It was a no-brainer!

We felt like we'd hit the jackpot. We were given free drinks all night and were showing off our best dance moves on the bar, and best of all — we were getting paid for it! We carried on that job every night for the rest of our holiday.

We didn't realise, but they had a camera pointing at the bar which fed into a big TV screen outside on the strip.

Men were walking past, seeing us and coming straight over, asking, "Can I buy you a drink?"

It's naughty really, but I'd go, "He'll get me a tequila" and the club would keep the money and the staff would pour me a shot of water. The bar owners were made up because they were making a ton of cash. It was my first taste of dancing, and I loved it.

If I was young, free and single, I'd probably still be on a bar in Zante dancing. Part of me misses that freedom in my life. I wanted to stay forever and be a dancer. I loved being over there. But we had to come back, because my sister had her partner to return to. I couldn't stay there on my own, so we flew home to Liverpool.

While my sister was reunited with her now ex-husband, I didn't have a partner waiting for me. Although, I did have a few boyfriends before I met Patrick.

After my brief romance with Michael in the first few years of high school, my first "I love you" relationship was at 15, with a boy called Adam. Looking back, I don't know if it was love, I was only 15 and it was the first time I had a proper relationship with a boy.

Adam was the popular lad where we lived in Halewood, and he used to be able to do mad things like run up walls. I remember he'd regularly run up the wall to my house at night and sneak into my bedroom after hours, unbeknown to my mum.

He was quite athletic and was so talented at martial arts. He looked like a man, and we just got on. He was quite cool, but I realised as the months went by that he was just a lad. I wanted more.

When I was 16, I started seeing another local lad called Leigh. He was a bit older than me. He lived in his own house and had a job, but he was wild and loved partying and that wasn't for me.

Then when I was 17, I met Alex. He was well out of my league and absolutely gorgeous.

It was the first time I'd met someone outside of Halewood. He was a model and signed to the same agency as me, and at the first fashion show — where we met — we played the part of a bride and groom. We even had a little peck.

But I was really scatty at the time; I was all over the place, this was in the middle of my partying days. We were in the changing rooms backstage and I couldn't find my phone, I was throwing all my stuff everywhere searching for it, there wasn't a calm bone in my body at the time. Alex came up to me and kindly said, "I'll ring it for you. What's your phone number?"

That's how he got my number and found my mobile for me. I wasn't looking at him thinking anything would happen or that moment was the start of a relationship, because he was just so gorgeous and lovely, whereas my previous boyfriend Adam was a proper lad from Halewood.

Alex was a gentleman, a model, and had his own plumbing business. His mum and dad were lovely, too.

After that night, I didn't think anything more of it until he started messaging me saying, "I'd love to take you out on a date."

That was strange for me because I'd never dated before. I'd never been taken out for dinner or ever gone to a cinema with a guy. Anything I'd had previously were just little bits of fun, but Alex was a proper gent.

We went out for a few months and he had a real family. And I just remember thinking, *I don't deserve this.*

He drove a nice car, and his mum and dad were so nice and welcoming. We never discussed my anorexia, but his mum would try and help me eat. She just had a way about her where she looked after me so well, but I couldn't cope with it.

He'd be talking about us going on holidays together when, in my opinion, I barely knew him. There was so much going on at the time, and all I could think was, *how can we plan a family holiday together?*

I found it weird that they all went on getaways together as a family, because that's something I'd never done.

His mum would say things like, "Christine, we're all going to go on holiday in the summer and you're going to come with us." I was like, *what, no way? I can't go on holiday!*

So, I broke up with him because I didn't feel good enough. When we split, he took it badly, and I'll always be sorry to him, and to his mum as well.

I'm sorry that I never really explained or talked it through, because I ended things over text.

I was all over the place and didn't think I deserved him, but I never said that to him. I just split up with him and that was it.

I'd never seen a family function like that before and it scared me a bit. Although it frightened me, it confirmed that's what I wanted in life. The way his mum and dad would look at each other… and they had a little boy and a girl! It was the perfect set-up.

When I look back, they were just a normal family. But where I come from everyone was from single-parent families, no one had their own businesses and barely anyone could drive.

All I wanted was a solid family with a mum and a dad. When I was meeting boys, it would always be, *is he going to be a good father to my children? Am I going to marry and spend the rest of my life with this person?* Because if not, it's not going to work out. That was my thought process from such a young age, and I think it has a lot to do with my upbringing.

The other man I should probably mention is Stuart. He was so similar to me, from the same area and we met at school. I always liked him, but I never would have had the confidence to approach him and it wasn't until we left school that we connected.

I guess we understood each other because we were both the poor ones in our class and our families were both a bit messy. He was raised by his dad and had loads of brothers. Again, he was a proper lad. I spent some time staying with him in his flat, and we still talk.

But we were mates and had a brief fling when we were teenagers. I knew we weren't going to get married and have kids, so I left it and that was the same with all of them. I wasn't looking for a bit of fun, I was always thinking, *if they're not going to be able to be the father to my children, then I'm not interested.*

All I ever wanted was to have a family with a good dad,

and I do believe you learn from your own parents' mistakes. Alex was the only one where I thought he'd be an amazing husband and father, but he was just way out of my league.

He was from a normal family, but I was blown away by it and found it too much. Then when I met my now husband, I was at a different stage of my life. When we first got together, Patrick lived in a normal three-bed house in Bolton, so it wasn't too overwhelming.

I wasn't like, *oh God, he's a millionaire!* It wasn't too over the top, which I'm glad of, because I would have struggled with that.

From that one detached house he owned back then, we went on to build our own home and we've gradually moved up the property ladder.

If I'd met him and he lived where we live now, I'd have probably run a million miles. What also helped me was that our relationship wasn't full-on from the start. It was a bit of fun that turned into a marriage.

But I definitely didn't love anyone properly until I met Patrick. Even then, it was a slow-burner to get to that point. I never expected to stay with him.

I guess I had my reservations about love and men after what my mum went through. She didn't choose the best baby daddies, bless her.

Although I have very little contact with my dad, my brother Jamie sees his father quite a lot. I'm pleased because that means at least one of us has a dad around.

It's sad and I do feel like I missed out on that dad-daughter relationship as a child. At school I was so envious of people who had a mum and a dad. Father's Day was always a tough one, too. I've never written a Father's Day card and would always bunk off school when it was coming up to that time, to avoid making one of those handmade cards.

Don't get me wrong, I had Mum, who was amazing, but I always felt like she was more of a mate than a mum. I remember as a teenager, my friends used to say, "I wish my mum was like your mum." But then I'd look at their families, where they had a mum and a dad together who worked and everything all seemed together, and I'd think, *I wish my life was a bit more like that.*

We were a bit all over the place and our lives were more chaotic. Mum had me when she was 19 and was always one of the younger mums at school. It was great at times, but sometimes I probably needed more of a mother figure.

As I've gotten older, in my twenties, and especially since having my own children, you realise how much your mum does for you. She'd go hungry to feed us and she'd take extra work on and do three different cleaning jobs to be able to buy us things.

When I look back now, I think, *wow, we really had nothing financially, but she always tried her best.*

She had her moments where she struggled, and having three young children – being a single parent with no money

– must have been incredibly hard for her. But we laughed through most stuff and we always had each other.

And where we grew up we didn't stand out, because it was the same for everyone. All the residents around there had next to nothing, and the mums in Halewood were just trying to get through life. I still go back there now, and you can sit in someone's garden and have a cup of tea. Everyone's got each other's back. Whereas where I live now, in Cheshire, I don't even know what my neighbours look like.

It's strange because I still walk around Cheshire and think, *I don't fit in here.*

But I do believe it doesn't matter where you've come from, if you're a good person then that's the thing that matters most. It doesn't matter what you've got, and it's something I instil into my children. No one should feel less in themselves.

You are who you are and be proud of that!

4

Pageant Life

Before I met my husband and had three children, I'd carved out a career in modelling. As I mentioned, my mum enlisted me into my first pageant at the age of 12. It was Miss Junior Merseyside, which to my surprise, I won!

After that success, I entered more and more competitions around Liverpool. I was always surrounded by gorgeous girls and the pageants especially were the worst for bitchiness and jealousy.

For me, taking part was never about winning though, to be honest I wasn't sure I even wanted to be there. But I just had to do *something*. More than anything else the aim was to help me like myself, because I didn't. My mum was trying to support me by getting me to mix with other girls and by giving me a chance to dress up and feel nice – but I just didn't. I hated myself. I didn't like the way I looked, and I never felt like I fitted in anywhere.

The other girls in the competitions had these amazing, gorgeous dresses, and there's no way I could have afforded one of those in a million years. My pageant outfits were either borrowed or from a charity shop. Whereas some of my competitors had these ballgowns that were worth thousands of pounds.

Another obstacle for me was the public vote. In pageants, they'd always have a poll open and whoever had the most votes via text messages, would automatically be awarded a place in the top three. It didn't matter what the girl looked like, how they spoke, what charity work they'd done, whoever got the most text votes bypassed the judges' scores.

I remember walking into rehearsals one day for a beauty pageant and all the girls were voting for themselves on their phones. I felt disheartened, because I couldn't even afford to have a phone. One of the girls was getting her mum, dad and brother to text in for her constantly and you could see the numbers going up on the scoreboard. I was desperately scrambling around for someone with a phone who could put in a few votes for me, just to give me a fighting chance. In hindsight it was an unfair competition and more about who had the biggest bank balance. It wasn't a great place to be and I'd leave feeling quite deflated, because I just didn't have any money at the time to compete with these girls. It felt like a losing battle.

I won a few titles, such as Miss Junior Commonwealth, but my biggest accomplishment in the pageant world was being crowned Miss Liverpool at 18. It was the third time I'd entered and I really didn't expect to win. The first couple of times I took part I was probably too young and I really wasn't that confident. But this time, I felt more prepared for it. Maybe it was my year.

Then it came to the dreaded dress. Actually, I was quite fortunate with this particular pageant because none other than former Miss Liverpool Danielle Lloyd lent me one of her frocks.

Danielle was on the books at the same modelling agency as me and I didn't know her that well at all, but her mum Jackie was big on the beauty pageant circuit and quite involved with them all. It seemed like Jackie wanted to look after me. She could see that financially I didn't have much, so she invited me around to her house and gave me one of Danielle's dresses to wear for the finals. It was one of the kindest things that anyone has ever done for me. Even though my confidence was on the floor it gave me a bit of a boost. I just thought, this is amazing, I'm wearing a celebrity's dress!

I wasn't expecting to win Miss Liverpool at all. It was all a bit surreal to be honest. My mum was sitting with my aunties at one of the tables and when they announced that I'd won, the auditorium was filled with shrieks. My family were all up on their chairs, absolutely delighted!

A Beautiful Nightmare

That night will always stick out in my mind. After winning the Miss Liverpool contest, I left the pageant life behind me. I'd already started to move away from competitions and modelling jobs.

My next career choice was where I really gained some self-belief and independence. And started earning some serious money for the first time in my life...

5

Nobody Puts Christine In The Corner

I've always been obsessed with the 80s film Dirty Dancing, and I mean *obsessed*!

As a teenager, I'd watch the dance sequences over and over again. I loved the music and wanted to be just like the characters Penny and Baby. So, I guess becoming a dancer in my teenage years was quite a natural step for me, and it was the closest I was ever going to get to my Dirty Dancing dream.

It was all about becoming a woman and I couldn't wait to grow up. I was desperate to start working and earning money and once I did, it felt like life got better.

It all began when another girl at my modelling agency

spoke about earning loads of cash as a nightclub dancer. She told me she was making more money than she ever did modelling. It immediately grasped my attention.

There weren't really many of those sort of clubs in my hometown of Liverpool and so she pointed me in the direction of Blackpool.

Obviously I already had a connection to the northern seaside town as that's where my dad lives, and I was keen to get involved.

I was offered work at a club, dancing, and I absolutely loved it. When I first went for the job it was minimum wage, but it was when men started putting money in my hotpants as I danced on the bar that I thought, *I can earn good money here* – it was easily hundreds a night. I did that for a summer.

It was such good fun and I felt like I was in the chick flick Coyote Ugly, as I strutted my stuff on the bar and men tipped me all night long.

During my dancing days, I was completely sober and was more than capable of taking care of myself. But I was so aware of the girls on nights out in the club I was working at. I was worried because of my history of bullying and my struggle to fit in among other girls, but actually everyone was lovely.

They'd say things to me like, "I wish I had your confidence. I wish I could dance like you."

I wasn't full of confidence at all, but it was a job I could do. It meant I could carry on my love of partying and music without getting involved in the drinking side of things, which wasn't good for me.

The other dancers were lovely and a lot of them were mums just trying to provide. Many of the women were going to university and needed to pay the bills, and there were girls like me who just wanted to make money and start a new life.

I managed to rent my own flat in Blackpool. It was my very own place and I loved it, but my God, it was grim. It was in the basement, had no lights, electricity or hot water. I was paying my landlord £200 cash-in-hand for it, which was ideal at the age of 17. And although it was not glamorous at all – it was disgusting in fact – it was mine.

I wasn't staying there much, anyway. I was dancing throughout the night and would sleep there during the day.

My move to France came about while I was dancing one night. A man approached me with his business card.

"You're far too good to be working in Blackpool," he told me.

"You need to be somewhere else. You need to go to Paris."

"OK then," I replied, in true Christine fashion.

I'd only been there a few weeks and so I rang him up, not really sure who he was or what he did.

"I go to a lot of these places and I think you should be somewhere else," he explained over the phone.

"I'll put you in touch with someone."

Life in Paris soon became addictive, I was making so much in terms of tips.

The dancing did so much for my confidence, too. In hindsight, what happened to me when I was 13 did affect me and stayed with me, but when I was dancing, I was in control. I'd taken ownership of my sexuality. No one was touching me and I was earning my own money – cash that went straight into my bank or back home to my mum.

While I was there, I was staying in a women's hostel with the other ladies who worked in the club. A lot of the other dancers were from eastern Europe and they were absolutely amazing, beautiful girls.

I got on with all of them and we were all there, hustling. It was just a good time. It wasn't a party or a piss-up, it was completely business. There were some ladies who were saving up for a wedding, or for their children to go to private school, while I was trying to raise enough money to buy my own house and a little car.

Sadly, there wasn't really much conversation between me and the other girls, because of the language barrier, but again I really wanted to fit in.

The place we were staying was quite run-down and we all shared a room together. And for the whole time I was there, which was over a year, I slept on a wooden bed, because that's what everyone else was doing. I thought it was because the hostel didn't provide mattresses, but I later found out they did! The girls just believed it was better for the body and their posture to sleep on a hard surface. I really wanted a mattress, but to blend in, I went against my instincts. Story of my life.

But we worked hard. We'd get picked up in a mini-bus at 6pm and dropped back at the hostel at 6am every morning. Then we'd sleep all day. I didn't really see much daylight while I was there, but I really didn't care because I was accepted for being me!

The only thing that got slightly out of control was my eating disorder. No one was keeping an eye on me, so I barely ate. I was dancing and burning a lot of calories, and I never took a dinner break.

It was easy for me to get away with not eating, because no one was watching me. I'd have a Cup a Soup, which was 90 calories, every other day and that was it. Nothing else, bar loads of water. So, it wasn't great for my health, but it was one of the happiest times of my life. I have no regrets, and at the time it was my own little rendition of my favourite film, Dirty Dancing.

I was still able to model, but when I went to Paris, the money I was getting for what I was doing was so much more than any modelling job. It didn't make sense for me to continue my modelling career and compete in pageants. I wasn't happy doing that, and there was bullying in that industry.

The money side of things wasn't great, either. You'd

go to castings where you were competing against 200 other girls. If you were lucky enough to get the job, you'd probably only make a couple of hundred quid, whereas I was earning so much more in one night at the club.

The modelling industry is fickle and you'd get picked apart if you'd put a bit of weight on, or your hair wasn't quite right. It certainly didn't help my plummeting confidence.

But dancing in the club was the complete opposite. I was in a place where I loved the music playing every night and I was working with a bunch of girls that I got on with and I was earning amazing money, and again, no one was touching me.

It was actually on a trip home from Paris when I met my husband.

I'd returned to Halewood to drop some money off to my mum and I got a call from my modelling agent.

"There's an event in Liverpool, please can you go to it?" she asked.

"I'm really tired, I don't think I can go," I told her. But she was persistent.

"Please just go, Christine," she said.

"It's a nice event – a tennis tournament, I just want you to do a bikini fashion show with the other girls."

And thank God I caved in, because that's where I met Patrick, at the age of 19.

By the way, I don't call my husband Paddy, I've always

called him Patrick, because that's how he introduced himself to me.

He was at the event with a mutual friend who I'd done a lot of charity work with, Dave.

Patrick wasn't too famous at the time. This was before he hosted Take Me Out and he hadn't done much TV at all. He was just a stand-up comedian and to be honest, even if he did have a thriving TV career, I wouldn't have known who he was – I was too busy earning to sit down in front of the telly. To this day, I've still not watched Peter Kay's Phoenix Nights or Max And Paddy's Road To Nowhere.

And at the time I was absolutely not interested in anyone. I was sober, celibate and focused on saving money for my future.

During a break in the show, Dave and I caught up. He pointed to Patrick and said, "I've got a friend over there, he's too shy to come over, but he wants me to give you his number."

Straight away I just thought, *if he's too shy to come over, he's not for me. I'm shy too, so it's not going to go anywhere.*

"I'll come and say hi in a minute," I told him. I didn't think much more of it and we carried on with the next part of the show. Before I left, I went to say bye to Dave.

Patrick was with him and said to me, "You looked amazing. You did really well. Are you coming out after?"

I was really trying to avoid going out and partying, so I declined the invitation and went home, but I took his phone number. I remember thinking straight away, *he's funny.* We had a laugh and that was it.

I arrived home and Dave must have given him my number, because when I walked through the door I had a text from Patrick asking, "Are you coming to meet us in Liverpool?" I deliberated but Nikki and her friends were out that night too, so I agreed to go.

I met up with Patrick and we spent most of the night just us two in a secluded booth, laughing. I didn't think for a second I was going to marry him and have kids with him. We shared a kiss that night, but that was it. The rest is history I suppose, but our relationship was definitely a slow-burner.

Things were really casual for the first few months. I'd go back to Paris and continue working and he lived in Bolton. But we always stayed in contact and met up when I was back home.

We just laughed all the time, and I adored his voice. His broad Bolton accent reminded me of my family in Blackpool. But there was no pressure on our relationship. He knew that I'd go off for a couple of months and then come back, and he was quite chilled about it.

And I suppose it gradually grew into a relationship.

I was happy doing my own thing, working abroad and definitely had no plans to move to Bolton.

After a while, he asked me, "Are you going to stop what you're doing in Paris and live here?" And I agreed.

As smitten as I was, it was really hard to move back, because I was so independent in Paris and I felt in control over everything. Even with my anorexia, although it's wrong, I liked that I could do what I wanted and no one was watching what I was eating. Although I accept that wasn't a good thing.

But it was really on my mind when he asked me to move in with him. I thought, *God, he's really going to see what I eat, or don't eat!*

I didn't want to give up all that money I was earning, either. But I wanted to be with Patrick, so I left my job in France and moved to Bolton. From Paris to Bolton – what a difference, eh?!

Little did I know quite how much my life would change when I made the journey back across the English Channel for good…

6

Troubled Twenties

When I moved in with Patrick, everything changed. And actually, I've realised while writing this book that I really didn't do much throughout my twenties, after I left the dancing world behind me.

Truth be told, I never really left the house when I lived in Bolton. I didn't know anyone there and Patrick was always away working. I slept a lot, watched a lot of daytime TV and of course barely ate anything. And other than the local supermarket, I never went anywhere. It's sad when I think about it, because I was in my twenties and should have been having the time of my life, but I was very lonely. I literally did nothing other than stay at home for years, waiting for Patrick to return from work.

Back then I had all the time in the world to be doing

things – no kids or commitments, other than looking after Patrick's dog Leah.

I didn't go to the gym, socialise or see my family. I definitely think I was depressed and would make excuses not to see my loved ones or go out. I'd gone from working in Paris and being independent and earning all this money, to meeting Patrick and really wanting to settle down and have kids.

I carried on doing bits of modelling here and there, but not lots.

One of the biggest jobs I got was my Loaded magazine cover. That was a bit of a dream for me. I took up the opportunity during the midst of my reclusive stage.

At first, my manager at the time landed me a lingerie photoshoot at Loaded.

I was really self-conscious and my body was beyond tiny. I remember not eating for days before the shoot, but I went and did it and it must have gone well, because within weeks the magazine got in contact again and offered me a cover shoot.

They asked me to go nude, which I didn't do, but we agreed I would shoot implied nude. Over my whole modelling career, I've never posed with my boobs fully out.

Looking at the pictures now, as a 33-year-old woman, I think the photographs are beautiful, but at the time I was down on life and not so keen. I'm so glad I did it, because it was a big deal and published in one of the most popular lads' magazines. But other than that shoot, which earned me a slice of cash, my modelling jobs were few and far between.

The thing is, despite my lack of income, I was able to take care of myself financially. People might assume that Patrick's always given me an allowance, but he actually hasn't. We've never had a joint account and all the cash I earnt from my dancing days in Paris is what got me through my twenties.

I've never asked him for a single penny.

Where it looks like I've not worked and not done anything throughout my troubled twenties, I had a massive chunk of money to use that I was very careful with, thank God. Anything I bought, or treated my mum with, any birthday or Christmas presents, I paid for out of my own little pot. And then, when it started to run out, I decided to go back to work.

I'm not actually a big spender, because of the modest background I've come from. I'm really shrewd with money, and I'm not materialistic. Don't get me wrong, it's lovely to be able to have a nice car and house and I have the odd designer handbag that Patrick has treated me to. He bought me one when we had the twins and on our anniversary for example, but in general pretty much everything I own I've purchased myself.

I still can't justify spending a lot of money on things and I usually buy high-street stuff. Other than my sunglasses – I love a pair of designer sunglasses – but that's it really.

However well we do in life, I'm not one of these people who buys a lot. Having said that, there's nothing wrong with it and a lot of my friends, and especially in Cheshire, have an allowance and that's up to them.

Even now I love earning my own money and that's always been really important to me. I want my children to know Mummy has a job too. I even say to them now and again, "Mummy's off to work." I've got two girls and I'm determined for them to see it's normal for both Mummy and Daddy to have a career.

I'm really fortunate with my husband's job, that he does keep our lives comfortable. He's provided a beautiful home and the bigger things in life, which I definitely wouldn't have been able to afford without him. But I love that if I do want something for myself, I can go and buy it without asking and that's something I never want to give up. It's independence and you can't beat it.

Anyway, during those years, I wasn't exactly rushed off my feet with work. I was mostly at home, doing nothing, while Patrick became busier and busier with his flourishing career in the entertainment world. He did various stand-in presenting stints on This Morning and The Paul O'Grady Show, but his first big job, which catapulted him from a comedian to a prime-time host, was Take Me Out. I remember when he got the phone call – we were engaged at the time and shopping in TK Maxx.

Of course, there was the initial, *wow, that's brilliant – my fiancé's going to be filming a TV show with 30 single women!* But I have to say, I was never really worried about it.

The show was all very tongue-in-cheek and fun. He stayed professional all the way through it and even though he could be a bit cheeky at times, he was never flirty.

I was probably more jealous of the girls getting to dress up and have their hair and make-up done. I would have loved to have done that show if I was young, free and single – although I would have been after the host!

That side of things wasn't a worry for me, but ironically the bigger his profile got, the more introverted I became. I was just at home alone and would do anything to avoid going out. It wasn't that I didn't get invited anywhere, I did, and occasionally I'd hang out with his cousin Lorraine, but I just couldn't face walking out the door. In hindsight, I think I was depressed.

His TV career went from strength to strength and I found myself feeling more and more isolated.

I had zero friends, I was in a new town where I didn't know anybody and his family and friends are a lot older than me, so I struggled to mix with them.

Patrick was riding his career wave and was probably buzzing because of how well things were going. He wasn't really thinking about how I was coping at home. He was living his best life and enjoying himself. I'm pleased he did, but it's very hard when you feel like you live a completely different life to your husband.

I was still obsessed with Patrick and absolutely adored him. It was just when I was at home, I was extremely lonely. For weeks and weeks, I'd have just myself for company, although we did manage to squeeze in a couple of holidays, even though – as usual – something always went wrong.

Our first trip was to Spain. We jetted off for a little weekend and I was really not at a good stage in my life. Being on holiday with a man was all new to me. I wasn't sure about it, but I went. We were in a swimming pool and I really wanted to recreate the Dirty Dancing lift.

He lifted me up and I sort of went over to go into the water and I cut my chin open at the bottom of the swimming pool. Then I had to go to the hospital and get stitches on the first day. After that I couldn't go into the water or sunbathe. I just wanted to be in Dirty Dancing and I bloody cut my chin open! So that was a fail.

Another occasion we went away to Dubai, which we didn't enjoy either. It was when I was pregnant with the twins. It should have been a magical trip, but it was one of our worst holidays.

We were nervous and anxious about the babies coming and it was the furthest I'd ever been away on holiday. I'd only stayed within the confines of Europe previously.

We booked it when Patrick's dog Leah passed away. It was his mum's dog he adopted after she died and he had her for about 15 years. We decided to go abroad because we didn't have any responsibility anymore and we were about to become super busy with the twins. It was our last getaway as a couple.

But Dubai wasn't what we were used to. We felt a bit on edge because we weren't sure what the rules were.

The hotel was lovely, though. We stayed at Atlantis, The Palm and to our surprise our room came with its own private butler. His name was Bonks. We didn't ask for one and we're not used to that lifestyle at all, but Patrick wanted to treat us because it was our last holiday for a while, although we hadn't anticipated quite how long that 'while' would become.

But it got awkward because Bonks, as lovely as he was, stood outside our room permanently.

He'd walk us to breakfast and when we went shopping he'd be following us.

Patrick thought he might as well make use of him. It was my birthday while we were away and he roped him into his secret plan.

He told him on the quiet, "It's Christine's birthday, I want to organise something special for her.

"When we're having a meal, can you bring her some flowers? And another day while we're here, can you organise for us to go and see the dolphins?"

"Yes, OK sir. I'll do it," Bonks replied.

Then came the night of this meal. We were eating and chatting and Bonks came over to me and presented me with this lovely bouquet of flowers.

"It's your birthday. From me, to you," he said.

I was like, "Ah, thanks Bonks."

When he left, Patrick said, "They're fucking from me!" But Bonks took all the credit!

Two days later we were lazing on the beach and Bonks comes over and says, "I've got a surprise for you Mrs McGuinness. I've organised for you to see the dolphins."

So, I said, "Wow, thanks Bonks, that's amazing." I'd always wanted to see the dolphins and Patrick knew this, so it was really sweet he arranged it all.

We got there and the place was deserted. It was just Patrick and I there.

Even Patrick was a bit like, "Wow, thanks for sorting this out, Bonks, this is great."

Obviously there had been some miscommunication or something, because Patrick had asked Bonks to book us in to see the dolphins – but Bonks had hired out the whole place for us!

And we were even more staggered when he handed us the bill – I think it was something like £12,000! We couldn't afford that at the time. And because I was pregnant, I couldn't even swim with the bloody dolphins. He'd hired out the whole place, sent Patrick the bill for thousands and took all the credit for it.

It's safe to say we've not been back since. We laugh about it now, but at the time we just didn't know what was going on.

Bonks was probably used to dealing with multi-billionaires who don't care how much it costs, but we just wanted to see the dolphins. It was probably the most expensive unwanted gift I ever had. Bonks cost us an absolute fortune!

When you come from an average background like we do, it's just not our life.

Back at home, living in Bolton just wasn't working for either of us, but I struggled especially. I didn't know anyone other than him and he wasn't there half the time anyway because he was commuting to and from London for filming.

These days we live in Cheshire, which we absolutely love and there's no doubt in our minds that this is where we're supposed to be.

Our move to this area all stemmed from me having a bit of a meltdown when the twins were one.

"I can't stay here anymore," I cried to Patrick.

"I'm leaving. You can either come with me or you can stay here, but I cannot live in Bolton forever.

"I just don't know anyone. I don't go out. I stay at home all the time while you're backwards and forwards to work."

It was a bit of a breaking point for us. And within a heartbeat, he replied, "Absolutely, what do you want to do? Where do you want to go? Let's get up and leave."

And within a couple of weeks, we'd upped sticks and moved into a rented house in Cheshire.

Initially, I didn't know anyone there either, but it was one of Patrick's friends that said, "Don't move to London, she'll still be on her own. If you go to Cheshire the train journey is an hour and 40 minutes to London."

My family are in Liverpool and an hour away, his family are in Bolton, which is an hour away, so we're still near all the people we need to be close to.

And since I've moved here my social life has completely changed. I don't know what it is, because at first, I didn't know a single person. People heard we'd moved into the area and instantly sent invitations to go to their house, to BBQs and their salons. It's a different life, and I feel completely settled here.

We've lived here for six years now, and we both say it's the best thing we ever did, for us as a family and as a couple. He comes home so much more when he's been away filming, because you can commute to London and back in a day.

We both agree that this is our home. It's brilliant, because I know everyone. If I go to the local shop, I bump into someone. I know all the parents at the children's school and I'm a member of a couple of gyms.

Before I moved to Cheshire, I thought it might be a bit cliquey, but it's one of the nicest places I've ever been to. Visually, it's absolutely stunning. I was raised in a big city, and now I'm surrounded by green countryside and the roads are empty – it's amazing!

We've since bought and renovated our own beautiful home. I'm glad we've stayed here, because it's a nice area and we don't stand out, as it's not unusual to see a famous face around town. There's quite a lot of footballers nearby. It's been the best decision for our kids, too. We got so fortunate with the children's school, which is just around the corner. It's not a specialist school, as such, but it's known for being particularly good with autistic children.

I looked at 12 different schools and there's nowhere suitable for our children like this one is. We came to Cheshire, knew no one and the kids are at the most perfect place for them. Moving changed our lives. I'm so glad he agreed to it when I had that meltdown, because imagine if he had said no!

But there's no denying my time in Bolton was really hard. Looking back, I wish I was into fitness like I am now, because I think going to the gym would have really helped my mood and given me something to do.

I never thought I'd be into the gym or exercise – it was never my thing at school. I didn't like PE and I wasn't part of the sporty group.

Even after having the children, my passion for fitness sort of came about by accident. I knew my kids needed to be around other children before they started school, so before I put them into nursery, I found a little crèche at the local gym, which I decided to take them to. It had a six-child limit, which was ideal for my kids who struggle with large groups.

At first, I was like this crazy mum sat outside the crèche, peering through the window to see what was going on. It was because they weren't speaking or toilet-trained at the time.

Eventually, it got to the point where I thought, *OK, the gym is upstairs, the crèche is downstairs – I'm in the same building.* They're happy and comfortable playing, so I might as well do something.

I remember walking into the gym and feeling like it was my first day at school. It was awful, I didn't know what to do. But I tried to make the most of the free time. There were even occasions when I took the children to the crèche and just went and had a shower and washed and dried my hair in the changing room in peace. I couldn't do that at home, because they needed to be with me permanently. That half-an-hour shower time was like heaven.

They got into the routine when they were in the crèche knowing the staff were there and Mummy wasn't. That was the first time I could leave the children in the same building, and I even made a couple of friends there. After a while, the kids were ready to go to nursery and school, and I carried on going to the gym during that time.

It just became routine. Now it is such a huge and important part of my life, and I say exercise is like therapy. It's not so much about body image for me. I don't want to lose any more weight, I actually go to the gym to gain weight. I want to stay strong and healthy.

And as any fitness freak will know, working out is so good for you. Mentally, physically, emotionally – everything.

Health is wealth, which is my motto these days. It's a shame I hadn't discovered this earlier, but I just wasn't in the head space during those years in Bolton to exercise. It was something I'd never been remotely interested in before.

There is a happy ending to the story of my troubled twenties. The beautiful part in my nightmare, if you will.

On Christmas Eve 2010, when I was 23, something quite amazing happened. I was sitting by the fire with Patrick and we were getting in the festive spirit and opening presents together.

In the middle of the excitement, he disappeared and seemed to be pissing about upstairs for ages.

"Are we going to bed then?" I asked him.

Eventually he returned to the lounge and presented me with a Christmas card.

'To my fiancée,' it read.

"I'm not your fiancée, you idiot," I joked.

And when I looked up, he was there with a stunning diamond ring – down on one knee.

There was no big romantic speech. No, "You're my world, you're my life."

But we're not really a lovey dovey couple. He kept it old school with a simple, "Will you marry me?"

I really wasn't expecting it, but of course I was ecstatic and said yes straight away. He must have previously told all his family, because the next day they were all around ours for Christmas Day and asked to see my ring.

I'd never really thought about marriage before. For me, it was all about having a family.

I had no big ambitions, like a ring, a Range Rover and a really nice home. I knew I wanted a car and a warm house. I wanted to be able to afford to put food on the table and for the children to have the heating on, because that was something my siblings and I didn't have as kids. My dreams weren't huge, I just wanted a mum and a dad together, a team and my own little family bubble. A solid family unit.

It's mad, because Patrick and I agree that on paper you wouldn't put us together. We're total opposites. He's a massive foodie and I'm not. He watches a lot of television and now I don't at all. We're polar opposites, but it just works.

And after that particular cheery festive period, it was straight into wedding planning mode.

As I took down the last of our Christmas decorations, I wondered what beautiful nightmares were ahead of me…

7

Becoming Mrs McGuinness

Six months after our engagement, Patrick and I were married on June 4, 2011, at Thornton Manor in Cheshire.

I was so happy to marry him. I couldn't wait to be his wife and become Mrs McGuinness, but the build-up to the wedding itself I found so stressful as it was a massive whirlwind.

We only had a short time to plan it, as the venue we wanted didn't have any availability the following year, so it was all systems go. We had just months to organise everything.

My weight was plummeting because, as you know, when I'm stressed, I don't eat properly.

I found it so hard even when it came to finding my dress, something that should be every girl's dream.

I just wanted someone to pick my gown, because I'm so indecisive. But I had no friends at the time to come dress shopping with me.

I had a real Pretty Woman moment when I finally went to look at dresses. You know the scene where Vivian, played by Julia Roberts, goes into the shop in Beverly Hills and the lady turns her away because she's dressed provocatively? Little did she know businessman Edward, aka Richard Gere, had given her a wad of cash to buy something 'elegant' with. Well, I had a similar experience.

I was passing this high-end dress shop in Cheshire and wasn't planning to go in at all. Because I was so thin, I was wearing baggy clothes all the time. I had this big tracksuit on, not a scrap of make-up and I looked far from glamorous. I never did in those days, and I must admit I looked a bit rough.

I walked in and the lady asked me, "What kind of budget do you have?"

"Well, I'm not really sure," I replied. "I don't know how much a wedding dress costs. I don't really have a budget in mind."

I meant that I didn't really have *a* budget because my husband said I could have whatever I wanted. But the shop assistant took it as I didn't have *enough* budget.

She said to me, "I don't think we're going to be able to

find anything suitable for you. These dresses are bespoke and they cost thousands." She then ushered me in the direction of a cheaper dress shop down the road. I was just so quiet and shy that I went, "Oh, OK then." I left the dress shop feeling absolutely awful. My confidence was at a real low and I was so stressed out that I just didn't know what to do next.

Eventually, I spoke to our florist who recommended another shop. There were a couple I liked, but not a dress that I absolutely loved. So, they put me in touch with quite a famous bridal dressmaker, Ian Stuart. He was brilliant and I was lucky that I could basically create my dream dress, which is ideal for someone like me who can spend hours picking between two white T-shirts. I chose the top of one dress, the bottom of another and the tail of a third and he put the design together.

I went for something quite timeless and I still absolutely love it. It was strapless, with a sweetheart neckline and diamantes around the top, ruched at the sides with a long train. It was absolutely gorgeous.

Although my fittings quickly became a problem. I was so underweight, because I was stressed and not eating, that every time I went for a fitting the dress had to be taken in.

I remember the staff ringing Ian saying, "Her dress needs to be taken in again." And he was on the phone going, "Her waist can't possibly be any smaller than what the dress is!" But it was and my waist was around 22 inches by my wedding day. I have to admit it was a stunning gown, and my husband and everyone absolutely loved it.

I'm sorry to say I didn't have a hen party, for the simple reason I didn't have any friends. It's sad, but true. I was so lonely at the time I actually thought that if it was my funeral, no one would come. If I had a hen party now it would be fun and I would have true friends there, which means so much to me after years of trying to fit in.

When it came to the wedding photographs, we were originally going to have the day covered by a big celebrity magazine. That was great because it meant they would provide a photographer for us, but days before our big day Patrick decided he didn't want to do that anymore. He wanted our wedding to be private.

It's taken years for me to figure my husband out and I'm still trying now. He works in TV and he's a performer, entertainer and comedian, and he seems like the life and soul of the party, but in his private life he's *so* private! He very rarely has people over to the house and he's not a show-off, which I like about him. He's a completely different person to the man everyone sees on the telly.

I struggle to get my head around how in public Patrick can be such a big personality, but in real life he doesn't like to have his photograph taken. It's a persona and it's his job. At home, he likes to keep his private life for just us. He's so particular when he does do photoshoots, that it's taken me a while to understand he's not being a diva. He'll insist on having a certain photographer and stylist, and he has to organise it. It's because he knows what he wants, as he's done this job for over 20 years.

In terms of my own career and public profile, it's been difficult to figure out the barriers and work out what he's OK with, while still making sure I don't hold myself back too much. I didn't realise the extent of how quiet my life was going to be when I moved in with him in Bolton, and he never wanted people over to the house. But now I'm in my thirties, I say, "I've got a friend coming round on Sunday, is that OK?" I need to have visitors over to our home; I've got young children and I want their friends over, too. It's a work in progress.

Anyway, just before our wedding we scrambled around for a photographer and at the last minute Patrick found one. We look back at the pictures now and both agree we don't love them. But it's just one of those things.

The day itself was overwhelming. I didn't really know anyone there, even though we had 200 guests! I didn't have any friends to invite and only 20 of the guests were my family.

I was worrying about everyone else, as a lot of brides do, and I struggled to relax and enjoy the day. I was also worried about people taking pictures, which my husband didn't want. And then there was the added heartbreak of my dad not turning up. So, I'm not surprised I didn't eat a single thing all day. But I imagine if I had been a guest I would have had a great time. It was actually on the hottest day of the year!

After getting married in the manor, our reception was in a big marquee by the lake. Rick Astley performed for us, although I'm ashamed to say at the time I didn't know who he was. But once he started singing, thankfully I recognised his music and was dancing away to Never Gonna Give You Up with my aunties, who all were starstruck by Rick. He's actually been a great supporter of us, and in recent years performed at our Twinkle charity ball.

It wasn't a big star-studded wedding, though. Other than Rick, the only well-known guest was Leigh Francis, aka Keith Lemon. Leigh is one of Patrick's closest friends and they genuinely do love each other. And Peter Kay was his best man. He had to be – they've known each other since they were kids.

Peter's speech felt like it went on forever – it was like a stand-up show. But the one thing he said that always stuck with me is, "As long as you've got laughter, you've got everything. And you two have got that."

It's so true and I say it all the time. It's become a bit of a mantra for me. Even during the most difficult times in our marriage and our lives, we've managed to laugh our way through.

The speeches were lovely actually, and one of the things that Patrick said during his speech had everybody in tears. He lost his mum before I had a chance to meet her and we had photographs of her on the top table, which was a nice tribute to her on that special day.

"Since I lost my mum I've had an empty space in my life, in my heart and home. But when Christine came along, it filled the gap that I've always had," Patrick said.

That was heart-warming, but I don't think I can replace that gap at all. I don't think anybody will, that's his mum at the end of the day. But if I can fill that void even a tiny bit, then I'm thrilled.

A funny story from our wedding day has to be the flowers. We went a bit over the top with them and the florist's bill was eye-watering! Just before one of the speeches, the flowers on the top table, which were near some candles, actually caught fire. We had to put them out quickly before anyone noticed.

When the celebrations had finished, we drove back to our home in Bolton. We were meant to be staying over at the manor, but we were worried about our dog Leah. We couldn't ask anyone to mind her because everyone we knew was at the wedding!

Despite all of the stress and chaos I was so happy to be married to the man I loved. The man who was to become the father of my children. The man I thought was the best thing ever.

While writing my book we celebrated our tenth wedding anniversary, which I can't believe! The time has absolutely flown by. We've had our ups and downs, which I'll get on to, but ultimately we love each other and I wouldn't want to be without the father of my children. Keeping the family together has always been at the forefront of my mind.

People always ask me if we would renew our vows, and I always say no because in our eyes we've done it once and we're happily married.

However, we never had a honeymoon, because just after our wedding Patrick was filming Take Me Out and another Saturday night show and he couldn't get the time off work. Then before we knew it, we had the twins and then Felicity.

In fact, we've never actually been away, just us two, since we've been married. Except on that trip to Dubai when I was seven months pregnant, which we didn't massively enjoy. So, instead of a vow renewal I'll settle for a holiday or, more realistically, just a few more cosy lunch dates in the not-so-distant future.

8

Our Little Twinkles

I'm so lucky to have three beautiful children. It's all the more special to me because looking back there were times I thought I was never going to be a mother.

Patrick and I were having regular sex for four years and there was never the slightest inclination that I was pregnant. I'd never been on contraception, and I was very aware that my struggle to conceive was due to my eating disorder. There were years when my periods were non-existent.

After some encouragement from Patrick, I visited a doctor. They told me I had polycystic ovary syndrome, which meant I wasn't ovulating enough to get pregnant. So, the goal before I started to think about having babies was to have regular periods. To do that I needed to eat healthily and most importantly, more food than I was. I was absolutely determined to be a mum and I thank God every day for the kids, because that is why I got better – I so desperately wanted to be a mother! It didn't happen overnight, and it took time to adapt to a healthy eating routine.

My husband would give me food in little dribs and drabs, so that I didn't even notice. It was in such a soft way. Instead of confronting me with a piled-up plate, like he'd have, he'd say, "Oh, try this." Although he never actually said anything, he knew I was struggling with my anorexia.

He started organising little Come Dine With Me parties, for us and close friends, because he knew I'd never eat in a restaurant with him. He was clever, because he'd figured out a way to get me to eat, where I felt comfortable. His brother and his partner would host an evening, and then his cousins would put on a meal. I think they knew there was a problem, because my dinner was always different to everyone else's, but it worked and slowly my periods began reappearing.

After we got married, we were actively trying for a baby, and were clocking dates in the diary and using ovulation tests. As men and women who are trying to conceive children know, sex on demand is not fun at all and can be quite gruelling. It's not like in the films, with rose petals and candles. You're sitting there with a calendar and an ovulation stick!

It caused us both a lot of stress.

The ovulation sticks in particular created problems.

For anyone who hasn't used an ovulation test before, the stick smiles at you to say you're ovulating and you have to have sex within the next 24 hours for the best chance of conception.

At this time, Patrick was away working a lot and we'd often miss the window, which meant we'd have to wait another month for the next opportunity. I'd get annoyed at him and then it became his fault.

Of course, it wasn't his fault at all, but I took out my anger and frustration on him.

It all becomes very clinical and not romantic at all. We both hated it. And then, after all the trying and struggling, along came my period every month which was a very unwelcome reminder that my body had failed again. It was all my fault. Then the cycle would start all over again.

It's weird, I spent years praying for periods and suddenly I was praying for them not to come, for that little glimmer of hope that I might be pregnant.

I'd never want to go through that time of my life again, and I feel for all mums who are struggling to conceive children. It was just awful. All we wanted was our own little McGuinness family.

One of the hardest things was when people questioned us about when babies were coming. Of course, it's a natural question to ask two people who have just got married. But behind the scenes, we were praying for a baby.

Everywhere I went, people were in shops pushing prams or were pregnant. I remember once getting really upset when I went back to visit my mum in Liverpool. I'd gone over to see her and she was decorating a crib for Billie-Jo who was expecting my nephew at the time.

"Will I ever be able to put a baby in a crib?" I cried.

You look at people holding their babies and think, *am I ever going to be able to do that?* And thank God it did happen for me, because it's all I ever dreamed of, becoming a mummy.

Of course, my life as a parent is completely different to what I expected, but I am a mum and you just get on with it. That's probably why I cope with Leo, Penelope and Felicity's autism so well. My children were so wanted.

People always say to me, "How do you stay so positive with three autistic kids?" But to me they're just my children and there's no love like a mother's love. I literally would do anything for them, because I wanted them so much and I still do.

So, you can imagine how thrilled we were the moment we found out I was pregnant with the twins! I just couldn't believe it.

It had become such a routine thing for us to do a test every month and every time I was left disappointed and defeated, so I was expecting the same thing again. Plus, I didn't feel any different. I wasn't tired, I didn't have sickness and my boobs weren't sore or tender.

Above: I was such a happy baby – and obviously enjoyed getting the practice in for my future modelling years!

Above: Aged around eight or nine. I found school challenging

Below: As you can see, I've always loved dancing! I had such a laugh with my friend Carla

Above: Despite the hard times in my childhood, I'd always manage to see the good in life. This is a picture from a visit to Blackpool, where I was born

Above left: A picture from my days dancing on the bar in Greece

Above right: Me and my dad on a good day. **Below:** My first newspaper article! It was lovely to get recognition for helping Carla

Award for brave Christine

By Jason Teasdale

QUICK-thinking Christine Martin proved she was a friend indeed when she stuck by her pal Carla France as she suffered a terrifying epileptic fit.

The girls were listening to music at Carla's house in Halewood when the seizure struck.

But brave Christine overcame her own fear, calmly comforted her friend and phoned 11-year-old Carla's dad to let him know what had happened.

It was only when they were travelling to hospital that Carla's mum, Marg, noticed Christine was shaking.

She said: "I can't thank Christine enough. I am sure that she has helped Carla through a very traumatic time despite being in shock herself."

"She shrugged off her own fear to help Carla pull through and I am very grateful."

Christine has now received a Citizenship Award from her teachers at New Hutte Primary School, Halewood. Head teacher Anne Johnston said: "Christine is a credit to her friends and family and a natural candidate for this award."

The Citizenship scheme, the brainchild of Lord Alton, is backed by Merseyside companies and recognises the good work done by young people in the region.

● Best pals . . . Christine Martin (left) and Carla France.   Picture: DAVE KENDALL

Above: I love spending time with my mum, brother Jamie and sister Billie-Jo

Below: Here I am in Faliraki at 16.
Nikki and I had a ball with these lads

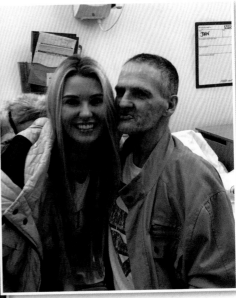

Above: Despite his difficulties, my dad has always kept his personality

Above: My go-to drink was a double-vodka and cranberry – one in each hand!

Below: I was so proud to land the cover of Loaded magazine in my twenties. I'm still glad I did it

My wedding day was beautiful – I couldn't wait to be Mrs McGuinness

Left: Patrick and I at our Twinkle Ball with close friends Leigh Francis and John Bishop. It was such a fun night and we raised lots of funds for charity

Below: I was so happy to have Mum by my side on my wedding day

Pregnant with the twins on the balcony of our hotel in Dubai. 'Bonks' the butler looked after us!

Top: Here I am with Mum, Billie-Jo and Jamie

Right: "If you've got laughter, you've got everything."

Bottom: I adored my bespoke wedding dress by the dressmaker Ian Stuart. I went for something quite timeless and I still love it

Left: Bringing the twins home was a magical moment

Below left: My little maths genius in the making, Leo!

Below right: Going to Peppa Pig World was a huge achievement for my kiddies in 2019. It was busy and loud, but they managed it so well

At that time, we were doing so many tests, which can be expensive, that I ended up buying some really cheap ones from Amazon. These tests don't say 'pregnant' or 'not pregnant', they are just a piece of cardboard with a line.

Anyway, I took the test before my time of the month was due. I did this often, because I wanted to get the disappointment out of the way, before my unwelcome period eventually arrived.

On this day, I left it on the bathroom side for a few minutes and then I saw it. The line was changing colour.

"PATRICK!" I shouted down the stairs.

He must have thought it was negative again because he came up and threw his arms around me.

"Aww. Are you alright?" he asked.

"Tell me, can you see something?" I replied, nervously.

The line was faint, because obviously I'd done the test so early.

I then went and bought one of the more expensive kits from the pharmacy, which confirmed I was two-to-three weeks pregnant. At that moment you couldn't get a happier couple in the world than us! Cloud nine is the best way I can describe it.

After all the trying and disappointment, we'd finally got what we wanted – a baby.

I booked myself in for an early scan and the midwife told us, "You've got two heartbeats."

Oh. My. God.

Patrick was crying and I was just in shock, even though I have twins in my family. I couldn't speak. It wasn't just one baby – two were coming along!

From that moment, I had this fear all the way through my pregnancy that I wasn't going to have them or something was going to happen. An overriding feeling that they were going to be taken away or something was going to go wrong.

From the beginning I thought, *there's no way I'm going to have these two babies.* I don't know whether I thought I didn't deserve it, but after that first scan, I went back for another two weeks later.

Then my worst nightmare came true when I had a really heavy bleed at eight weeks pregnant. That was horrific.

At that time, Patrick was away for a couple of nights filming in Manchester and he'd asked his cousin Lorraine to come and stay with me. He didn't tell her I was pregnant, but she must have thought something was going on. Inside, I was so excited. I was constantly cleaning the house from top to bottom, and I suppose I was nesting and not realising.

I was just really happy and floating on air. I don't know if I'd done too much or what it was, but during those couple of days I just flooded with blood. It was everywhere.

I rang Patrick, inconsolable.

"I've lost them, I've lost the twins – that's it, they're gone," I screamed.

Somehow, he got to Bolton from Manchester in what felt like five minutes.

I was crying saying, "I can't flush the toilet." I was convinced the babies were in there. He then phoned the hospital who'd just scanned me.

"There's no way," they assured him.

"She might have lost one, but both heartbeats were there and everything is normal."

Sometimes you can bleed during pregnancy, but there was just so much of it, I was convinced they were gone. They told us to wait until the next day before going to hospital, because I wasn't in pain.

"Let's see if the bleeding stops, wait 24 hours and then come in for a scan," they told Patrick.

So, we waited, but of course we didn't sleep a wink that night. The next day we made the journey to the hospital preparing to be told we'd lost the twins. We got in there and the room was silent for what felt like forever, before the doctor said, "They're fine. They're in there."

Through tears, we asked, "Both of them?!"

And they told me my beautiful unborn twins were still in my tummy, hearts still beating.

It could have been my womb having a clear out, but it's just one of those things you don't know about when you're trying for a baby.

After that, all the way through the pregnancy I was on edge. I was convinced something was going to happen to them. And I think that explains why when I had the children, I wouldn't let anyone near them.

I was so over-the-top protective. Now I think, *oh God, I was actually quite rude to family and friends* and I wouldn't let anyone hold them. I wouldn't even let anyone take a photo. I was so petrified of losing them. It still stays with me now as a mum. That feeling of, I've lost my twins – I'm still not over it.

You hear how common miscarriages are as well. People said to me, "Oh, you're having twins. They might come early or they might be underweight and have to go into ICU."

Again, I was mentally preparing for this stuff that never actually happened. Physically I was tiny. When I got pregnant, I was only around seven stone and at 5ft 10in, I was very underweight. But during my pregnancy, and especially after that bleed, my maternal instinct kicked in. I've never eaten in my life like I did in both my pregnancies. I devoured everything possible and foods I'd never tried before. I was determined to be the healthiest I could be, because I had these babies inside me and I wanted them so badly, so I had to get well.

Thankfully, I carried them the whole nine months, with no problems, other than that terrifying bleed. I ended up having a C-section, because I had no signs of labour. They clearly were so snug where they were, so on July 2, 2013, I was booked in for the procedure at St Mary's in Manchester.

First into the world was my baby boy, weighing a healthy

6lbs 7oz. We knew we were having a little boy and a girl and decided to call our son Leo, after Patrick's star sign.

I wanted something with a link to Patrick and I was thinking about calling him Patrick Junior. My husband didn't like that, so we thought Leo was the perfect fit. His middle name is Joseph, which is Patrick's middle name after his late father.

Then there was Penelope, who arrived a minute later, weighing 6lbs 10oz. I wanted a really girly name, but not anything too eccentric or unusual. Penelope was really pretty and it wasn't too common among little girls at the time. Her middle name is Patricia after Patrick's mother.

They were both beautiful and Patrick and I were so smitten. It was a slice of heaven. We had a son and a daughter, we'd hit the jackpot.

That newborn baby stage is amazing and you can give me that any day.

My C-section was really straightforward and I was home the next day. But then I started going into full over-the-top protective mode.

Patrick went back to work four days after they were born. He was already in the middle of filming a really big Saturday night show and he couldn't have any more time off, even though I'd just had two babies. I should have had someone with me really, but I refused.

I became an expert at saying, "No, it's fine. Honestly, I'll do every nappy, every bottle, you go to work. I'll be a stay-at-home mum and this is how we're doing it." I made those rules. It was me who said, "I'm quitting everything – I'm not modelling anymore. I'll stay at home with the babies."

So, I did everything. It wasn't his fault; I wouldn't let anybody else help. I insisted on doing absolutely everything.

Because the babies only spent time with me, and with Patrick when he was at home, when they did see anyone else or if someone popped in, they would scream the place down. Or even if the doorbell rang or the coffee machine bleeped. Obviously, I now know it's because they're autistic, but at the time I thought, it's because they're just with me and they don't know anyone else.

If anyone looked at them, they'd cry, so I'd tell people not to. I wouldn't let anyone near them. When I tried taking them to baby groups, they couldn't cope with it, so I stopped going. The health visitor would come round and ask, "How are you? Are you getting out and about and seeing your friends?"

"Of course I am," I'd lie.

When in reality I was just in the house with my babies, permanently.

Tesco was the only place I felt comfortable taking them, because they'd be asleep in the trolley.

"Oh, your twins are so good!" everyone would say to me.

But now I know it's because of their speech delay. They should have been babbling or giggling, but I didn't notice they were behind because I'd spent years in the house with them, not knowing what babies their age were supposed to be doing.

I didn't have any friends with young children, so I thought they were developing absolutely fine and I was just obsessed with them. I didn't realise they were missing these milestones.

I was an over-the-top protective mother. And now my mind's clearing, I know it was too much.

But they would have struggled if I'd tried to give them a normal life and take them out and about. They wouldn't have been able to cope with it, because they can't cope with it now. I think staying in, just me and them, actually gave them an easier childhood.

One day I found my mum crying in the garden. She'd been staying with us for a couple of nights and had obviously spotted the children weren't where they should be.

"There's something not right with the twins," she told me. "They're not developing right."

So, I agreed that I would take them to a paediatrician, who told me that they were just delayed in their development because they're twins.

Looking back now, the signs were there. They weren't eating solid food, they'd spin on their tiptoes, there was no eye contact, and they'd line things up... Normally, a paediatrician would have picked up on that. But I never flagged those symptoms to her, because I never thought in a million years it was a sign of anything bigger.

I couldn't wait to tell my mum the good news. I was so relieved.

After that, no one really said anything. But if they did, I had that answer from an expert. If anyone had flagged it, I could say, "They've got some delays in their development because they're twins."

I introduced them to a nursery when they were around three. And if I wasn't pregnant with Felicity, I don't think I would have ever taken them. But I was expecting and exhausted. I thought, *I've got to do something and they're going to go to school soon*. I'd leave them there for 20 minutes while I waited outside the room, and I could hear them screaming. I'd just sit there and wait. I did that for months and months.

It was when they started nursery where I really saw the gap between my children and others. When I took them into the busy room for the first time, I saw the other toddlers eating with a knife and fork, putting their own coats on and chatting away. These children were having conversations and mine couldn't say a single word – they couldn't even say hello. I didn't realise kids of that age were meant to be having full-on chats with people.

I was so protective of my children, I wouldn't let anyone say anything about them anyway. But if anyone was to point out, "Why aren't they doing this or that?" I'd have been the first person to say, "All children develop at different stages."

It's mad because we really didn't do much in the first few years of their lives, but we didn't know why.

Things like baby groups, they'd scream the place down. I took them to a little musical group called Rhythm And Rhyme and they didn't like it one bit. I thought it might be because they were too young, but now it makes sense that the drums and tambourines that other children were playing with, for my children it was really painful for their ears as they're so sensitive to sound. And for me I dreaded the thought of potentially having to mix with other mums and socialise. That filled me with anxiety.

Weeks would go by and we wouldn't see anyone. I just got on with it, because that was my life at the time. It's not like I'd given up a life of partying, I was already at home all the time anyway. I loved them to bits and was obsessed with them straight away. I was extremely protective. I used to hate anyone even holding them. I don't think I could believe they were even mine.

I'd be petrified of my health visitor coming over and telling me I was doing something wrong, but they just fitted in with my life at home. I wasn't as lonely anymore. It was a lonely life anyway because I didn't have any friends, but I had my two little mates, my beautiful twins – our twinkles as we called them.

The twins starting nursery was an eye-opener. That's when I thought, *when these children start school, they're not going to be able to cope.* It took a long time for me to be able to leave them at nursery fully after years of it being just me and them. I had to build it up really slowly.

It started off just at just 20 minutes a time, then it became an hour and then eventually two. I had to work around meal times. I would give them their breakfast, take them in and then bring them home for lunch, because they wouldn't eat there.

I remember on one occasion I'd dropped them off at nursery. At this stage I'd never even left the car park. At the time Leo would only eat this one type of butter, and we'd run out. I was terrified that if I didn't get this butter Leo wouldn't eat his toast. And it's true he wouldn't have. For the first time, I left the twins at nursery while I drove to three different supermarkets on the hunt for this bloody butter.

I couldn't find it anywhere. I cried my eyes out in the middle of the supermarket. Now when I think back, alarm bells should have been ringing. That's not normal. But for me I was just doing anything I could to get my child to eat and I'd do it again tomorrow if I had to.

The more the twins were at nursery, the more I felt comfortable talking to the staff about their speech and the fact they didn't recognise their own names when called.

I'd go and pick them up and I'd see other children running with their arms out going, "Mummy," whereas my twins seemed oblivious to the rest of the world.

They'd be sitting there spinning objects and doing things they did as tiny babies. They were still having bottles and wearing nappies. They wouldn't play with Play-Doh, sand

and slime. They couldn't go outside without ear defenders on.

I didn't see it as being any different, because they'd always been like that. But when they were in nursery, I realised the way they played with toys wasn't how other children played with toys. Your average neurotypical child would roll a toy car along the floor going, "Brrrmmm." But Leo and Penelope would be twirling the wheel over and over again or be carefully examining how it was made.

The nursery also noticed something wasn't right, but they never said the word autistic. Yet they did help and told us they could apply to get the twins speech and language therapy.

From there it snowballed into, "Let's get Early Years Foundation Stage into the nursery to help support them."

And before I knew it, we were sitting around a table with eight different adults from different sectors of child support, preparing them to go and see this paediatrician. Still, no one said along the way, "The reason we're doing this is because they're autistic."

But I never asked the question. I just thought, *oh they need help, so let's get them help.*

Even when I was taking them to the hospital for food therapy, which I'd never heard of and had never seen anyone doing, I never questioned it. I never thought, *why am I in the hospital two to three times a week for appointments with my children?* I just believed I was doing what I can as a mum to help them and this is what the professionals are suggesting, so I'll just go along with it.

I was heavily pregnant throughout all the twins' appointments. Eventually, we saw a paediatrician when they were three-and-a-half, before they started school. The assessment went on for hours and it was just awful. It was a really clinical environment. They had strangers asking them questions, asking them to play with toys that weren't quite toys, so they could see how they interact with certain things.

They took note of all their symptoms, such as walking on tiptoes, lack of eye contact and sensitivity to noise and textures, and they questioned us extensively about their development. As the day drew to a close, the twins were understandably exhausted and unhappy.

"Right, I'm going to take the babies home now. Can we follow this up with another appointment?" I asked the paediatrician.

"No, I need to speak to you about the results from today's assessment," she replied.

The twins were screaming, so I said, "Right, can we be quick, because I need to go home."

Eventually, she broke the news to us that they were autistic, in as simple terms as that. I cried my eyes out.

I was convinced she was wrong, because I didn't know anything about autism. I thought, *what's she on about?* There's nothing wrong with them. They're fine. Because in my head, I thought she was saying, "The children aren't what you think they are." But she wasn't.

I'd seen all the symptoms she was talking about, but I just saw them as my kids, I didn't see them as 'autistic'. I was really upset. I thought, *she's telling me there's something going on here and I can't see it, when I know my children better than anyone. I've spent pretty much every minute of every day with them. I know my Leo and Penelope better than she does!*

But it wasn't that at all. It was all these things like how quirky they were and their sensitive personality traits, like they didn't like noise, bright lights, or strange people – all these little things that she's saying is autism are the things I loved about them.

So, once I got my head around that, and that being diagnosed as autistic doesn't change them, I was fine with it. They were still my beautiful children, who I adored and was obsessed with. They were always autistic; I just didn't know.

I believe it's so wrong the way the news that your child is autistic is delivered to you from a paediatrician. It's so down and depressing, but once you understand it, you see it's just a part of their personality.

I wish we could have gone away after the assessment, returned just Patrick and I on a different day and properly discussed it with the professional. But we just went home in tears, thinking it was the most awful day ever and not really understanding what we'd just been told.

It's a shame, but the way the system is in the NHS, there's no follow-up appointments, no advice on what to do next, what it means for them and us now… We had to just go off and research and learn about autism ourselves. It's just awful. It's something that the NHS are trying to change, and I think it will develop into a more thorough diagnosis and subsequent follow-up appointments over time.

Luckily, the twins were already referred for speech and language therapy and food therapy, because the nursery had picked up they were behind in their development. In terms of advice on autism and what happens next there was nothing, sadly.

My husband struggled with their diagnoses more than me. He saw it as quite a negative thing and he had therapy to deal with it. More than anything he craves normality and worries about their future. But he's finding things easier as they get older.

And the spectrum is so huge, that there are so many different kinds of autism. There are lots of different symptoms, too. Some are mild, some severe. Sometimes it can make sufferers quite disabled, where they're not able to feed themselves, change themselves, use the bathroom, or sleep at night. It comes with quite a lot of mental illness as well.

But I've never seen my children as anything other than my children. I want hidden disabilities to be normalised, and for people to recognise them in others.

We'll have to explain to the children at some point they're autistic, but we just don't know when or how.

There are a lot of children's books that can help, and I'm wondering whether to read one to them and maybe they'll go, "Oh Mummy, I'm like that character!"

Or, if to wait a little bit, because they are still so young. I've met a lot of families when filming for our BBC documentary about autism with my husband. Some of them said they've spoken about it openly with their children since they were young and that they've never had to have a conversation, the kids just always knew they were autistic.

There were some parents that had left it until later life, when their kids were teenagers, which seemed to go pretty badly. They struggled with it a lot more and didn't like the label.

For us, it's finding the right moment. I don't think there is a perfect age, the twins are now eight and Felicity's five, but it's just going to be a 'right time'.

They might hear us talking about autism one day and ask us what it is, and of course we'll be happy to explain it.

It's something we'll have to consider and I'm positive about their future.

But during those first few years of having the twins the sheer volume of appointments and worry was relentless. I still don't know how I did it. Things then got a whole lot busier for us, because two months before their diagnoses, my whirlwind Felicity arrived...

9

Three Is The Magic Number

Things were difficult with the twins and I was constantly toing and froing to appointments, so Patrick and I were deliberating whether to add another child to our family.

As well as Penelope and Leo's autism battle, there was my fertility to consider. From the day I'd given birth I hadn't used any contraception, and no baby had come along in the first couple of years.

Patrick and I spoke about it and he said, "If you want one more, let's just see what happens.

"I don't want to go through the whole marking dates on the calendars, but if we do want one more, let's have a cut-off point."

He was in his forties and didn't want to still be having kids in his fifties, which is understandable. And he hated the regimented sex schedule we had when we were trying to conceive the twins.

"If we have one more, then great. But that's it," he told me. And I agreed. And much to my surprise, when the children were three, I fell pregnant with Felicity.

The nine months I carried her were really straightforward and I've been lucky with both my pregnancies that I didn't suffer badly. Although the twins didn't understand there was a baby in Mummy's tummy, because they were both completely non-verbal at the time.

I was nervous about having my C-section with Felicity. Not the actual procedure itself, but it was the first time I'd left the twins overnight. I was so worried about them I wasn't thinking about me, or anyone else. It was all about how the twins would cope without me when I go and have this baby.

I'd planned it all out and arranged for my mum to come over to look after the twins. It was the first time she'd stayed overnight alone with them too and in my mind, I was thinking, *I'm going to be home tomorrow, it's just one night and Patrick can go backwards and forwards between home and the hospital.*

But in beautiful nightmare fashion, things didn't quite go as planned. After the procedure on September 9, 2016, they didn't bring Felicity straight to me once she was out of my stomach. At first, I didn't think too much of it, because a similar thing happened when I had the twins and it was 45 minutes before Leo was eventually put on my chest. I actually held Penelope first and all I could think about in that moment was, *where is Leo?*

Patrick explained to me that my precious son was having a couple of breathing problems, but he was fine. Still, it was the first 45 minutes of his life that I lost and that was hard enough.

But with Felicity, I was there for hours without her. It felt like forever. Where was my gorgeous baby girl?

I'm not sure how long the process was. Once the baby's out it's usually around an hour to completely stitch you back up again, but it felt like it had been forever.

Then when I was being sewn back up Patrick wasn't around at all. Neither was my baby, so I knew something wasn't right.

Eventually my husband walked in the room.

"She's OK, she's OK," he told me.

But he didn't actually know what was going on himself.

Patrick sat down with me and then the next minute I saw this trolley whizz down the corridor. The nurses paused and said, "This is your baby, we just need to take her to intensive care."

I was staring at them and asking why.

"We need to go, we'll be back in a minute," they replied, and off they dashed.

I cried my eyes out. They had to concentrate on helping her and that's fair enough, but I'll never forget that feeling of having no bump and no baby.

Time ticked away, before someone eventually came and explained to us Felicity was having difficulty breathing and needed some support in regulating her temperature.

They weren't sure what it was, but they needed to take her to intensive care.

Because of my C-section, I was numb from the waist down, so I couldn't get up to go in a wheelchair, even if I wanted to. I sat in that room desperately praying for my legs to work and to be able to feel my body move so I could get up and see my baby. But I couldn't. I was stuck in my bed until I could walk. I couldn't see my beautiful girl.

Eventually, they wheeled me to my own little room and Patrick went in to see Felicity. I still hadn't held or seen her.

He took some photographs and came back to me and said they were tending to her, because they thought she might have pneumonia. Thankfully, she didn't, but they were treating her for that, just in case.

I didn't understand it fully, but a lot of the symptoms she was showing can indicate pneumonia. It was all mainly precautionary, but it was still extremely worrying and upsetting and I wouldn't wish it on anybody. All you want to do when you have a newborn baby is hold them, and I couldn't.

It wasn't until later on that night, when I was physically

able to move, that they put me in a wheelchair and took me to her and let me feed her the first bottle. I instantly fell madly in love. She stood out by miles among the premature babies in the intensive care ward, because she was massive!

Among these tiny newborns was Felicity. Lying there at 8lbs 2oz, she was huge. But my little girl was just amazing from the minute I picked her up and fed her the bottle. It was the best thing. And with all three of my children I felt that way. I felt so lucky that they're my babies when I first saw them. And still, every single day I gaze at them and think, *God, I am so lucky that these are my children*. They are incredible.

Despite the fact Felicity was all wired up, which was awful to see, I was just so glad I could hold her.

I know now Felicity had a condition called shock lung. It can happen with a C-section when a baby comes out instantly, they get a bit shocked by having to breathe on their own, so they had to give her a bit of support.

It's something that always stays with you. I remember thinking about Leo, that I'd missed those first 45 minutes of his life and that I didn't hold him at first, but with Felicity it was a whole day I lost out on.

In total, we were in hospital for four days, mainly because when a baby is given antibiotics at that age, they have to stay in to be monitored. All the while my twins were at home, more than likely wondering where their mummy was.

While we were in the maternity ward, Patrick kept returning back to the house to check on Leo and Penelope. Once he'd settled them into bed, he'd come back to the hospital to see me and Felicity and then go home overnight.

At night my darling girl was still in the intensive care ward and I was in this hospital bed on my own with an empty crib next to me, which was awful, but I was just so thankful she was OK and alive.

Bless her, she needed oxygen because she couldn't breathe without it. She had to regulate her temperature on her own and that's what she was struggling to do. It was just awful, but on the last night they said she could stay with me in the room. I was ecstatic.

She was so chunky and perfect, with really dark hair. I couldn't wait to take her home. The whole experience had been difficult for everyone.

We called her Felicity, mainly because we thought it's such a lovely, pretty name. It suits her so much as well – my Felicity. Her middle name is Rose, after mine.

Other than severe reflux and her autism, she's had no other health problems since. But she's caused drama from the very first second she was born. She's full of personality, strong and just full of life. Everyone who meets her, loves her. She's wild.

Then came the long-awaited moment we took her home to the twins. We carried her into the house in her car seat full of anticipation, but to our surprise Leo and Penelope didn't even look up. They didn't acknowledge her. Even when she cried, nothing. It's probably a blessing, because I was worried the twins would feel really left out, like most siblings would. And don't forget, they were used to life as just us.

They didn't notice her or take it on board because they're autistic. They didn't have that connection there that there's this new family member and there was no excitement from them, which is quite sad. You'd expect a little girl and boy to come running over to a baby, but they didn't. There was nothing. It wasn't that they didn't care or love her, it was just at this time, they didn't understand what this new baby with their mum was.

It wasn't until Felicity was about one, when she was crawling about and stealing their toys and biscuits, that they noticed she was there.

Despite the fact they're autistic, they are still siblings at the end of the day and have their moments, but they've become really close. Especially over the pandemic, and particularly the twins. People used to say to me for years, "Are they really close?" And I'd think, *no, they barely even look at each other!*

They never seemed to have this bond, but now it's so strong between them all. There's no mistaking that these three children have grown up together.

Within six months of having Felicity, we knew she was also autistic. I spotted the signs from the twins and I was much more educated about autism and knew first-hand what the symptoms were.

She started tensing her whole body, which babies can do anyway. In fact, a lot of symptoms of autism can be prevalent in non-autistic children as well, and that's why a lot of kids get diagnosed later on.

But we knew there was a risk with Felicity and the signs began to show. She'd get so excited and she'd be looking at me laughing, tensing her whole body and clenching her fists.

Oh God, here we go again, I thought.

We kind of expected it and were more prepared for it, but from then on it was just one thing after another.

Her hand movements were quite different and milestones like sitting up, crawling and making sounds were all delayed. And when she started walking, it was on her tiptoes, which is quite common with autistic children.

Even now, if Felicity has nothing on her feet, she'll walk on her tiptoes.

We knew deep down a diagnosis was coming, so I put her in nursery when she was one, which is a lot earlier than I did with the twins. I knew that if she was autistic, it could potentially affect her social skills and speech and being comfortable playing with things such as paint and sand.

I was worried about her not getting enough socialising at home, whereas if I put her in nursery, she'd be around other children and she'd get used to the noises.

I didn't want to leave her that early, in fact it broke my heart, but it was being cruel to be kind. I just knew how much mixing with others had to become a part of her life. It wasn't enough for it to be just me and her in the house, and it definitely made a difference to her development.

Easing her in was the same process as the twins. I'd sit outside for 20 minutes at a time. I nearly gave up after two months, because she just wasn't settling. I was so close to saying to the staff, I'll leave it a couple of months and come back. But eventually she did get used to it there and got really comfortable. It is awful leaving your children with someone else, especially when they're non-verbal.

She eventually got diagnosed when she was three-and-a-half. Her speech was delayed and she had all the usual symptoms. Her diagnosis was quicker, because when we were talking to the paediatrician, we knew what we needed to point out. It was quite obvious and the doctor could quickly see she was autistic.

Although the process wasn't as difficult as it was with the twins and we knew it was coming, you can never prepare yourself for it. It still hits you quite hard and it's just as upsetting. However, when we got the diagnosis, there was a part of me that was relieved that I wasn't imagining it and she wasn't just copying what the twins were doing.

Patrick and I travelled to the appointment in separate cars, because afterwards he had to dash off to work and I had to pick the twins up from nursery. I cried the whole drive from the clinic to the nursery. It's not that I personally mind that my children are autistic, but it's the worry for them – that they might get bullied or that their life is different and they think differently. Although they don't know it, because they don't feel or realise they're unlike any other children.

My upset has always been over the concern for them. There have been loads of times where they've misunderstood things. For example, going to and from lessons at school can be challenging for them. They have to have a visual calendar that they learn from. It's great we have those things in place to support them, but at the same time it flags up that they're not like other children if they're relying on picture cards to see when a lesson starts.

Once Felicity was diagnosed, it cemented in our minds that our family is complete. Patrick and I always wanted four babies, but with three autistic children we knew we had to draw the line there. Not because we were worried about a fourth child being autistic, but the children we have need so much of our time and care. Life is already so full-on and we're pushed to the limit. We love them and I wouldn't change them, but to have another one and take time away from our three babies that really need all the support and attention we can give them, it would have been for us, not them.

So, in 2019 my husband had a vasectomy, which was a hard decision for both of us. It still bothers me. Deep down I always wanted one more, so emotionally it's been difficult, but mentally we knew it was the correct choice. We're so lucky with our three gorgeous children. Three is the magic number after all.

10

Meet My Beautiful Children

As you may know, my husband and I have never put our children's faces in the public domain.

It's nothing to do with their autism. Even before they were diagnosed, we never shared photographs of them. My husband never wanted to show the kids publicly, and I do agree it's the right thing. I'm not saying I'm keeping them out of the limelight forever. If the children would like social media when they're older, then that's up to them. But while they haven't got a say, we've chosen to protect them in the best way we know how.

So, although I can't show you my babies' faces, I'd like to tell you all about them. Here goes...

Firstly, it amazes me how the children have all got the same diagnosis, but are completely different in personality.

While all three of my children struggle with socialising, my son is more outgoing than Penelope, who battles with anxiety and isn't too comfortable mixing with others.

Leo loves to jump up and down and gets really excited sometimes. The technical term is 'stimming', so he stimulates a lot. He's got a real passion for mathematics, but is particularly obsessed with spinning objects and loves anything round. Leo's always loved toy vehicles – cars, planes and trains. As a small toddler he'd sit and spin the wheels for hours. From a distance, you'd think it was just a child playing with a toy, which is most likely why his autism went unnoticed for a while.

But when I look back at old videos, I see that he'd sit and examine the wheels and want to know the mechanical side of everything, which is a sign of autism.

Although my husband struggled to come to terms with the children's diagnoses and spent very little time with them in the first few years of their lives because he worked away from home so much, he and Leo really do have a special bond now. I really think it comes from their mutual love of cars. I have to say, one of the best things to come from my husband's career is his presenting gig on Top Gear.

He got the job offer just after we went through our difficult patch – more on that later – and at the time there was very little connection between my husband and our children. But his work on Top Gear instantly meant there was something he could bond with Leo over.

When he started production, Patrick was getting different cars dropped off every week to test out for the show. One week it would be a Porsche, the next a Ferrari, and then a Volkswagen Polo.

Leo would get so excited every time a car would get delivered, because he absolutely adores anything with four wheels. It doesn't matter to him how expensive the car is, he'll just be excited about the different shapes or colours.

That's another thing I love about my children – they don't have any concept of value. They could have free rein to choose any toy in a shop and they'd pick up a bouncing ball. It's really amazing. They're not spoiled and just love the little things in life. So, you can see why Leo gets just as excited about a run-of-the-mill motor as he does an exotic supercar. A car is a car to him.

Patrick's job on Top Gear has been so beneficial for our family, because that was the first time he felt his son wanted to be around and play with him.

I could see the elation from him instantly. He loved taking Leo out for a spin in the different cars, and that was the first time they'd spent quality time together. It's still so lovely to see.

The change in my husband as a father has been amazing to watch. Now, he gets and understands the children. He knows how to deal with the meltdowns, what to look out for and how to distract them if he thinks one is brewing. He's really grown into an amazing dad. As a man and a dad to the kids, he's brilliant and I couldn't ask for any better. Having three children isn't an easy life – it's challenging and exhausting. But he's got used to it and it may have taken him years, but it's got to the point where he can have the kids on his own now and again.

And as much as Patrick has a special bond with Leo, the girls love him so much, too.

I'm so pleased for them that growing up they're going to have a dad there for first dates and parents' evenings. That's all I ever wanted. I never had that bond with my father and my children are so lucky to have a dad that loves and cares about them and provides. He's a good role model.

Alongside his autism, Leo has other health issues to contend with. Unlike the girls, he has some vision problems and wears glasses. Because of this, he has appointments at the hospital every six weeks to get his eyes checked.

He's also got hypermobility, which means he's really bendy and his joints are quite loose. Physically, he's not very strong, which is something he might need help with when he's older. He can run, walk and play, but he gets tired quite easily and his limbs go everywhere when he's moving, so he has physiotherapy and support in school for that.

Probably the scariest of Leo's health issues is his severe nut allergy, which is quite frightening for us, because a peanut could potentially kill him.

We first discovered his allergy on a trip to the zoo. Because it was a big day out, the children were all quite anxious, so I let them choose a chocolate out of a tub of Celebrations as a treat.

After eating the tiniest Snickers bar, Leo turned ghostly white and was struggling to breathe. An ambulance came out and luckily, he was fine, but that will always be a worry for us.

Personality-wise my little Leo is so fun, caring, full of energy and funny – they're all funny and have me laughing every day. Out of the three children, he probably struggles the most with his meltdowns. He can't control them.

If something goes wrong in his day, he will throw himself on the floor and have the biggest meltdown and it's difficult to snap him out of it. It could be something small like the doorbell ringing, or the toy he's playing with breaks.

Leo's meltdowns were at their worst during the lockdowns – they became physical. He started lashing out at me, Patrick and the girls, and physically hit and kicked us. He was hurting himself, too. It was awful, because they've always had meltdowns, but never physical like that.

It's difficult, because I love my children so much. I tell them every minute of every day, and overly smother them and try to make life as fun as possible.

I just want them to feel loved. But when an autistic child is having a physical meltdown, you have to switch from being a parent to a carer. You have to detach from the emotional side, make sure the other children are safe and try to calm them down as quickly as possible.

It was heartbreaking to see, and I know he'd never want to hurt us, but it's an emotional outburst they can't control. Thankfully it's been better lately, but it was super tough to go through as a family.

And Leo's change in behaviour wasn't the only problem we had to endure over the pandemic.

My eldest daughter Penelope told us she didn't want to live anymore and asked about going to heaven.

As a parent, you can never prepare yourself for those types of conversations – my seven-year-old daughter crying in my arms every night saying she doesn't want to live anymore. It was heartbreaking.

It's scary because, although she didn't mean it and she doesn't understand death, and that you don't come back, it's worrying to think she could do something or try to do something when she doesn't realise the severity of it.

It was an issue I had to talk to her about and I really didn't want to. It was during a conversation one night when we were all in lockdown and she hadn't seen anyone else other than me, her siblings and Patrick for months.

She was desperately missing her one-to-one teacher at school, who she's very close to. She also couldn't understand why no one could give her a hug anymore and why we had to stay away from each other.

It upset her to the point where she took it very personally.

So, I had to explain to her, "This is for everyone. These rules are for everyone. Mummy isn't allowed to hug anyone either."

Eventually, she did go back to school and I spoke to the staff about it and her one-to-one agreed, because she was having regular Covid tests, she felt more than safe and comfortable to give Penelope a cuddle if she needed it. That really helped and thank God, I haven't had to have any of those conversations since. She's settled back into school and she's doing OK, but now we're struggling to get her back out of the house.

For example, she absolutely loves horse riding, but she's just refusing to go.

Unfortunately, it's something that's really common with autistic children and adults, and especially teenagers – they can be overcome with anxiety about things. It's something I'm always going to worry about with Penelope, as she's prone to feeling very overwhelmed.

It's so hard as a parent to see that all three of the children have regressed in lockdown. Regression can happen to autistic people, and it's usually triggered by a change in routine or event. But that doesn't make it any easier when you've spent years building them up to do things that don't come naturally to them.

We're hoping that Penelope will have the confidence to start getting out and mixing again, but it's going to be a slow-burner.

She's a very sensitive little girl and always thinks of others before herself. Often to the point where she worries too much. She loves animals and has become so attached to our cat Millie (Millie has a willy, because he's actually a boy – a stray cat we recently adopted.)

Now she's in school, the biggest worry with Penelope is the social side of things and mixing with other children isn't something she finds easy. She tends to go off and play on her own quite a lot.

We're just trying to find the right balance of allowing her to get the alone time she needs, because that's fine, but making sure she isn't completely isolating herself. But I don't want her to feel like she has to be with other people, just because the other kids are. I want her to be herself and if she needs quiet time, then she should have it. It's something we're trying to find a balance with.

Then there's my whirlwind Felicity. Let's put it this way, you know when Felicity's in the house!

She'll throw the biggest tantrums, but she'll also give you the most laughter. She's a full-on personality that I've never come across before. I'd say Felicity is a mixture of both the twins. She's really caring, loves her dolls and lining things up and is very strict with her routine.

She can be very social and confident, but then she's selective with who she's with and it's important she feels comfortable with who she's around. Felicity's a very independent young lady.

I feel she was more ready for school than what the twins were. It just shows the difference it can make when autism is diagnosed early on. Just by knowing what to do and being patient and understanding that things will get better. If I hadn't had the twins, I don't think Felicity would be doing as well as she is now.

In a way, I'm glad I had those blissful years of being unaware the twins had autism, because I didn't have all those extra worries. They were just my children – I loved them and they were perfect. And they still are all of that, but because I knew Felicity was autistic from an early age, I didn't have that time without the extra concern.

With Felicity, from the beginning I was thinking, *oh God, I'm going to have to go through all of these therapies again* – the paediatrician appointments, doctor's appointments, starting nursery and school, and all the worrying. But then again, I'm glad I knew sooner, because she's doing amazing now because of the support she's had from the beginning.

One of the hardest things about their autism is their food aversions, and all three of my children suffer terribly with them. It's common among autistic people and it can last all through their lives; some people get better, some don't, some get worse.

For all of my children it's sensory. It can be the smell, colour, taste or feel of the food.

Leo also has problems with his routine. If his routine changes, that will affect his eating as well. He didn't eat any solid food until he was around three-and-a-half, and it's been really limited since.

All of them eat nearly entirely beige food. Most of the time it's fries, chicken nuggets and toast. Penelope will occasionally have pizza, but that's the most adventurous food any of them will try. There's no lasagne or Bolognese. On Christmas Day, I still served them up the standard chicken nuggets and chips. Even though it might be the same meal every day, and it's not the healthiest, I'm just glad to see them eat. They're really particular, and I've spent years worrying about their health.

With their autism I think, *well, at least they're still healthy and happy*. It's just they have these other issues and struggles. But for Leo, his issue with food does affect his health. In the past, he's been very underweight. At one point during lockdown, we did discuss with the doctors about putting a PEG, a feeding tube, in his tummy. That was so hard. We never did it, thank God, because we found these milkshakes full of calories which built him up and his weight has been better since. But it was so difficult even having that conversation and discussing doing that to a child who is fully able to eat – mechanically everything works, but he does not want to put the food in his mouth. It's heartbreaking, because your child is starving.

Leo doesn't even like touching the food, so I have to pick it up and put it in his mouth. It can take him an hour to have a piece of toast in the morning. They all have it cut in a particular way, but with Leo it has to be bitesize squares, which I pick up and feed to him or he just won't eat. He doesn't ever ask for food.

Obviously, his issues with food are similar to mine as a child. I would avoid meals at all costs and I still find it hard to remember to eat sometimes. I think that's why when everyone was panicking about the eating situation with the kids, when I used to go to food play therapy with the children, I'd think, *well, I wouldn't want to eat it either.*

But for me it spiralled into an eating disorder, which I'm very conscious of with my children – I'd never want them to go through that. I guess it's kind of a sensory eating disorder for Leo. It's just part of his condition. I'm hoping it'll get better as he gets older and thankfully, he is touching more foods now.

I'm always sensitive to the fact they might not want to eat and they might not like it, but I also don't want to make them poorly. We just try to make our meal times fun. We get them involved and don't make it into a big deal how much food they've had, while making sure they are actually eating.

It's difficult, because Patrick works away a lot, so we barely eat together anyway. When he is at home he'll eat alone, because he's actually, unlike our kids, a real foodie. I'll be busy feeding the children, so I'll grab something as and when I can and most of the time on-the-go.

We've never eaten in a restaurant as a family and I don't

think they've ever had a meal outside of the house – even a picnic.

One takeaway cuisine the children do love is McDonald's. It's quite popular among autistic children and adults, and that's because it never changes. The fries are always in a red box and the food always tastes the same. It's beige and dry. You can find McDonald's all over the world, so there's that familiarity there.

When we looked at going abroad with the children, the first thing we said was, "Let's check if there's a McDonald's nearby!" No parent wants to give their child too much junk, but when they're struggling with solid food, you'd literally give them anything. They really do let themselves go hungry if you give them food that they're just not going to eat. You know when people say, "They won't starve." But these children actually would.

If it's not food they're comfortable with, they won't eat it. That was another problem with lockdown – when McDonald's closed. I was like, "Oh my God. They're not going to eat!" I ended up putting out a message on social media and had thousands of people saying they felt the same. I was so lucky that McDonald's sent me some of the red boxes, which was an absolute lifesaver!

As you can see, there are so many little obstacles we have to overcome on a daily basis. But I guess the biggest difference between us and other families is that we're limited to where we can go and what we can do.

It's really hard for me to scroll through social media sometimes. It's upsetting to see parents posting about holidays with their children, or taking them to football practice or after-school clubs. I struggle to watch videos of their children out playing, just doing normal things, because ours don't really do that. The reality is we're at home a lot.

It's not that they can't go out and do things, it's just finding the right activities. But the world is so limited. As much as people are trying, and places like soft-play centres are putting on autism hours, there is still a long way to go with it and they need to make it more accessible.

It's not autism-friendly if they're organising the session twice a year, or at 7pm – when it's quiet, so they're not losing any money. In reality, that's not helping us. They need to have a regular session at a normal time. I'd love to find a weekend class or group, maybe something sporty, that all three of them can go along to. They are capable of doing it, but I need it to be quieter than usual and that's what I'm struggling with. It doesn't necessarily have to be just for autistic children. I just need there to be around ten children attending, not 30.

But it's not all doom and gloom. Yes, there are a lot of concerns and struggles, and my children need a lot of support, but there are so many benefits to having this hidden disability.

My children really are *so* intelligent. Both Leo and

Penelope are getting mainly A-grades at school, which is incredible and I'm so proud of them. While Leo loves talking about numbers and needs a lot of praise, Penelope quietly excels. She adores reading, and her English is very good. For a little girl who didn't start speaking until she was four, she's doing incredibly well.

We don't know where Felicity's passion lies yet and what she might be extremely good at, but all of the children are very artistic – the girls especially. Penelope has a photographic memory and she's able to just look at an image and draw it with all the details spot on. They are much more intelligent than what I think they would be if they weren't autistic.

Felicity's memory is insane. She recently saw a baby playing with a rattle and she said, "Oh Mummy, I had that rattle when I was little, didn't I?" And I just thought, *how on earth can she remember that?!* They all love music as well and they can memorise the lyrics to so many songs.

Felicity developed a stutter during the lockdown. It was quite severe and it literally came on overnight. She'd trip over every single word, but I'd put songs on and she could sing along perfectly clearly.

Music is something we all love, actually. One of my happiest times is when I'm driving with the tunes playing. It's like therapy for me, and I love it when I get a spare half-hour in the car. I always take the long route home from dropping the children off at school. It really is my me-time.

The kids sing along in the car, too. We play a lot of old-school R&B, and they love a bit of Bob Marley and John Legend. We can play the same song over and over again. At the moment, they're enjoying Celine Dion.

But their absolute favourite song is the Liverpool FC anthem, You'll Never Walk Alone by Gerry And The Pacemakers. I think the lyrics are so apt for my children. They'll never walk alone, and I fully believe that. Music is therapy, and I was raised with it playing every day in the house. I think it helped my mum get through really difficult times, and it's been a big support to me, too.

11

Mammoth Milestones

When my children were diagnosed with autism, I did go through a bit of a grieving period.

Your hopes and dreams for them slightly shatter, because their future is so uncertain. Most of the time when you have children, you expect them to go to school, college, university and then get a job. They then might get married and have children. But when you've got autistic children, all of those things aren't for sure. You just don't know what path they'll take.

Are they going to have a career? A relationship? Their own family? When the children were diagnosed with the condition, it was something we had to get our heads around – we potentially might be looking after our babies after they transition into adulthood.

Financially, we might be supporting them beyond adolescence, too. I think that's one of the reasons my husband works as hard as he does, because we could be subsidising our children for a long time. That's something we both worry about. We work that bit harder and earn that bit more, because we know there's a good chance we're going to have to fund our children's future when they're adults.

All we can do is support them now, while they're younger. I believe investing in them now will help in the long run. We try our best to push them out of their comfort zone, but cautiously.

It would be easy for us to live a quiet life, isolated in our gorgeous Cheshire home, but I always knew my children could do more. They deserve it, too.

Having a holiday abroad was never going to be easy, but my babies did it.

We never took them away when they were super small because we knew how much they struggled with change, lights and the sounds of different places. The last thing we wanted to do was take them out of the house, just so we could have a holiday.

My husband would have his own getaways, but we never actually went away to another country as a family of five until the twins were six and Felicity was three.

It's something you have to consider when you have autistic children – am I doing this for me or am I doing it for them? Are we pushing them too much to go on holiday because *we* want a holiday? When actually, they don't. They're quite happy staying at home where everything's familiar.

But then you think, if we don't encourage them, they will just stay in their little comfort zone forever and I wanted them to experience a holiday. If they enjoyed it, then we knew we could do it again. So, we gave it a go.

Don't get me wrong, it took a lot of preparation. There was a whole year's worth of build-up to get them in the best position to take them on one of the most challenging obstacles they'd ever faced – getting on an aeroplane.

But with all the determination I had, I began my mission impossible. I started off by taking them to an airfield almost every weekend to get them used to the sound of the planes.

To protect them we'd put their ear defenders on, so they could cope with the noise. The first time we went, they wouldn't get out of the car. But as the months rolled on, we took them to the car park to watch the aeroplanes. Then the next step was to take their ear defenders off, so they could get used to the sounds of the jets.

Once that proved successful, I arranged a date for them to have a walk around a static aircraft. It was like a model plane, really.

Meanwhile, I had to prepare them for the big task of stepping foot on a beach. Their feet are really sensitive, hence why they walk on their tiptoes so much, so again that was a big hurdle for my three autistic children to overcome.

I figured that if I could decrease their sensitivity to things they're going to come up against while on holiday, it would make it easier when we got there.

We started with a little pit in the garden, and the kids played with the sand. That was a huge milestone, because this was something that they would never do. They wouldn't normally touch it, let alone play with it.

Then I took them to a play centre, which had a sand pit. Before going to a shopping mall, which had a mini beach inside. I also took them to a water park, which would prepare them for the swimming pool and sea.

It was a full year of constant work to get them used to doing things that were kind of like being on holiday before we actually booked anything. And then, when we felt like they were ready, we planned a getaway in the UK. We organised a flight from Manchester to Southampton, where we planned to stay over for a weekend.

We wanted it to be a short flight, in case it went wrong, or they didn't want to get back on the plane home and we'd be stuck there not knowing what to do. If they couldn't cope with it, at least we had the option of driving back. It was our little test flight.

But it was a huge thing. They had never stayed in a hotel before, let alone eaten in a different place without their usual cups and plates. With my children, continuity is everything.

And, as expected, it wasn't smooth-sailing – or flying, being more apt. When it came to boarding, they were scared and anxious. Leo had quite a wobble before he would get up the steps to the plane. But they DID IT! And once we'd ascended, they were fine. Then when it came to staying in the hotel, something we were nervous about, the kids were actually excited.

Their routine had changed so they didn't sleep well, or eat much, but they had accomplished the biggest experience of their lives, which was stepping foot on an aeroplane.

As they'd conquered their fears, we booked to go to Spain a little while later.

Again, we organised a weekend mini-break, but there's no denying it was a more difficult trip. It didn't feel like a holiday, like what other people have. It was really hot, much busier, the flight was longer and we were in a foreign country where there's a language barrier.

But for the first time in their lives, they walked on a beach. That's a memory I'll have forever.

They were six and Felicity was three and they'd never stepped foot on sand before, other than the small man-made beach at the shopping centre. They were feeling anxious and they wouldn't go in the sea, but they played in the sand, made sandcastles and went swimming in the pool at the hotel. They did *so* well!

They didn't eat much, which is something that tends to happen when things are different, and they didn't sleep very well either. But they had a little holiday, and I think they enjoyed it.

Saying that, it was a hell of a lot of prep for a weekend, and the flight was hard. We couldn't relax for a minute. We just knew when that 'bing bong' noise to call the air steward over went off again, it could trigger the children to jump out of their skins. The airport was such a stressful environment, too.

We haven't been away since, but we will try it again. The pandemic stifled a lot of plans for everybody and when it comes to going on holiday again, I fear we're going to have to start the preparation process from the beginning. It took so long to build them up to overcome those barriers of even being near a plane, so for them to actually get on one was massive.

It was a really big achievement for them to play in the sand and have fun on the beach. I suppose it's one of those things that people take for granted when having children. You have your little holidays and it's a normal thing to do, but it took us years and it's something I'll never forget.

The positive we can take from their condition is that there have been so many amazing milestones we've marked together. Just hearing them speak is incredible, because they were silent for so many years.

It was a tough road to get them to where they are now. When they were non-verbal, I communicated with them by using pictures.

I had a clock in my house with photographs around it explaining the time of the day and what was next on the agenda. When it was lunchtime, I would point to a picture of a plate of food, or bedtime there would be a bed. I'd show them a photograph of Nanny when she was visiting.

I also used a lot of emoji symbols, so they could point to them to tell me how they were feeling.

Getting them to speak confidently was a long slog, but I was overjoyed when they could say "Mummy". Penelope said it first, and she was faster at saying single words. Leo was silent and then when he started talking it was full sentences. I also used Velcro to spell out words for them to pronounce. It started with "Mummy" and then I would spell "I love you, Mummy".

We'd point at it every night and then eventually I added "night night". So, that's how we did it. "Mummy", "Daddy", "please" and "thank you" were their first words. They're really polite and amazing kids, which is something you can't buy. No matter where you come from, being well-mannered is everything. They're more than I could have ever asked for, and I'm glad they are the way they are.

They say "excuse me", which is so cute. I never asked them to do that, so it must be something they learnt at school.

It's great. Because of the added help of their speech and language therapy, they've come on loads and now, if anything, they're too verbal. Even when they're arguing with each other, I jump for joy inside, because for so long they didn't say a word.

When it comes to their emotions a lot of people think autistic people can't feel them, but I believe they can. When the kids are arguing, they are showing feelings, which is great.

They all say "I love you", and I fully believe that they mean it. I'm sure when I say "I love you" to them, they know that they are loved and wanted.

It was something we had to teach them, as those kinds of emotions don't come naturally. Building friendships and relationships is also a challenge, but it's something they really have to work on.

They're doing amazing, but they still need support and aren't doing what other eight and five-year-olds are. They're getting there, albeit slowly.

When they started eating solid food, that was a biggie. Again, an accomplishment for us, but some other parents see it as a given.

That's the fabulous thing about it – Patrick and I get to celebrate so much with the children.

One of the greatest things for me was when they started wearing a wider variety of clothes. They are still very particular about the clothes they wear, and whenever I get them new bits for their limited wardrobe, I cut out the labels. They don't like the feel of them and they can find it itchy on their necks, which is a sensory thing. I can totally relate because I'm exactly the same and have been cutting the labels out of my clothes for as long as I can remember.

They won't wear anything with seams in, and I have to check socks before I get them to make sure they're soft enough. It's just been a part of life for me.

Over time, they are getting a little bit easier with what I can buy. In the past, everything had to be completely plain, but now I can treat them to the odd T-shirt with an image on the front.

There were years when I'd be out Christmas shopping and see all these little girls' dresses with sparkles and sequins and big skirts. I'd look at them and really want to see my babies in them. They're just normal party frocks, which most little girls wear – but mine just wouldn't.

These days, they are more likely to. But only if I put a T-shirt underneath and the dress isn't touching their skin.

Starting school was a huge accomplishment and something I'm so proud of, because I wasn't sure if they ever would. I just didn't know where they would fit in.

Because of my experience at school, I wanted to get it right for them and I feel like I have. They seem really happy.

Their school is lovely, but every day I speak to my children's one-to-ones to make sure they're playing and socialising.

Kids can be cruel and with them being autistic, while for me it's not a big deal at all and it's just who they are, it's something the other children could potentially pick on.

Bullying is something I worry about, especially because of what I went through as a child. But I'm hopeful that children nowadays are more open-minded and understanding and hopefully mine won't have to deal with that. But you just don't know, and it's something I'll always keep my eye on.

But for now, they're thriving. Each year, Leo and Penelope participate in the Christmas play. They've got better every time, but there's always been a little hiccup.

The first Christmas, they sang Twinkle Twinkle Little Star and didn't last longer than two minutes before having a meltdown. The twins started belting out the nursery rhyme, then they saw all the parents and me and that was it, they wanted to leave. They were holding their ears and were upset, because it was too loud.

The second year, they had a speaking part and managed to stay involved a little bit longer, before something happened with Leo's costume. He walked out and then Penelope wanted to leave, too.

Then, last year, they did the most they've ever done in a school play. They sang, were speaking and stayed on stage up until the very end.

But just as the show was finishing, Penelope had a little meltdown. She had fairy wings on and another child was tugging at them behind her, quite innocently. She lost it and then left.

So, we haven't got through a whole show yet, but it's

amazing they're even doing it. And I've got high hopes for even better this year – and of course Felicity will be there to add to the fun.

Another win happened really recently. This year, the twins really wanted a birthday party. I was dubious, because deep down I questioned whether they actually did. We'd previously thrown them little ones before, and it didn't go too well. They usually think they want something, and then it gets too much. But then I thought, *who am I to stop them from doing it, when they are telling me they want to?*

So, we went for it and it worked. Don't get me wrong, it wasn't a stereotypical kids' party, but they had a big bouncy castle, a teepee and a few friends round. There were six children in total, and I'd brand it a success.

I also took them to one of the first events thrown since the last lockdown ended. I decided to go with all three of them on my own, which is a rarity in itself. It was a children's live entertainment show and I was debating whether to go for ages, but I thought, *I need to, I need to get them out. I'm just going to do it.* We'd been stuck indoors for so long, I had to get them out of the house.

The worst thing that could have happened was that one or all of them would have a sensory overload, but I reassured myself that if that happens, I'll just pop them in the car and we'll go home.

It was brilliant and they loved it. I think it went so well and was relatively pain-free because every family had to be in their own pod due to the Covid restrictions. It was almost like a pen where you herd sheep.

That may seem really odd and bizarre, but for us it was perfect. I don't think my kids would have been able to go to that event if it wasn't for those little rules you have to stick to.

While I don't know what the future holds, I'd like to carry on taking them on little outings like that if we can. It'll just depend on what is suitable for them.

There have been a few stumbling blocks along the way, but persistence is key when it comes to building my children's confidence up.

Things like going for a dentist appointment, or even a haircut. Those everyday, ordinary things that to other people are just routine. For my children, it's a huge deal.

It took years of visiting the same hairdresser with Leo, before he'd sit in the chair. He couldn't stand the noise and the sound of clippers on his head. It's all sensory. It would be a traumatic experience every time we'd go, but I had to keep going and keep the routine.

I've always taken them to a salon in Cheshire that's just for children. It's great because they have toys, books and little iPads they can use.

They always knew Leo needed extra time, because he'd be in floods of tears, so they booked a longer appointment for him.

I'd put it on his calendar every four weeks, so he knew it

was coming. It took years of perseverance and now he will go. He'll still fidget a little bit, but he will sit and have his hair cut.

It can be hard sometimes, just doing normal things that other families do. Things like taking them swimming – now they love it, but it's taken years to get to this point.

Everything was a problem. Going into a busy changing room, going into a cubicle and having to close the door to get them changed… that could trigger a meltdown because for them, it was scary. There was the noise aspect, too. The swimming pool area can be quite echoey, and that would petrify them.

It's things you'd see families doing all the time on social media. You see everyone taking the kids to the swimming baths, but it was always awful for us.

And then they wouldn't eat because they'd be somewhere different. I think that's probably one of the worst parts of how autism affects our family, the things we can't do. We're getting there, though.

It's great to be able to support them in their development. I spent so many years being at home, being a mum and not going out. My focus was 100 per cent on them.

It still is now, but I juggle work and have a little bit of my own life sometimes.

For the first five years of their lives, it was just me and the children. Everything was about them and their appointments. I feel lucky that I've been able to do that because my husband works so much. I've met other families where both parents work, or they are single parents, and they've got autistic children. It's sad hearing that they're not able to go to all the speech, language and occupational therapies, and sensory play.

They're juggling work, and I'm really fortunate that I've been able to put the time in.

I do think early intervention is amazing for autistic children.

I've definitely seen a big difference in Felicity getting help at a much younger age than the twins, and I'm sure that will continue.

You can probably tell I'm super optimistic about the children and their future.

While I always look at the positives in their autism, not everyone shares the same sentiment, and we've come across a lot of prejudice along the way.

12

Dealing With Diagnosis

"I bet you wish you didn't have children," someone once said to me.

How disgusting is that! I couldn't believe it. Well, actually, no, they're still my children and I love them so much and I'm so lucky to have them. I don't introduce my kids like, "This is Leo, Penelope and Felicity and they're autistic." They're just my babies.

Don't get me wrong, their autism has been difficult to deal with. While I feel upbeat about our children's future, Patrick feels quite down about it all and struggles to see the positives in their condition.

The first time my husband talked about their condition publicly was during an interview with fellow comedian John Bishop in 2018.

He'd never spoken about it so openly before and that's mainly because he struggles to. But Patrick agreed to do the interview with John, on his In Conversation With show, because he's a close friend of ours and he's met our children.

"It's still very difficult for me to deal with," Patrick said on the show.

"Very difficult. I crave normality with my children. Honestly, John, whether they were autistic or not, I'd like to think I'd never be a parent who was putting pressure on my kids to be a bloody brain surgeon or a dentist. it wouldn't matter to me if they worked at Morrisons or what they did, as long as they were happy, because I was happy growing up like that.

"Now, I have this different thing. I was out at the local supermarket and a guy was there with his son. And he's going, 'Dad, can I have a yoghurt?' 'No, you can't have a bloody yoghurt, your mum's doing your tea.'

"I looked and thought, *God, that bloke's so lucky to have that.* That's how I felt at the time.

"With certain paediatricians, there's a scale, and it's like, where are you on the spectrum? The autistic spectrum. They're saying that's gone now, there isn't a scale, but I believe there still is.

"You can walk into a room with a child with autism, and it can be very extreme and you can spot it straight away. That child may be doing something like rocking backwards and forwards, be non-verbal, sensory, touching things with their tongue… you can instantly see it.

"And then you could go into another room, with another child with autism and they'll be sat playing with a toy, and you wouldn't think anything of it. Then all of a sudden, they could burst out into tears and have a real meltdown, because that toy isn't quite doing what they think it should do. It's a really tricky one to deal with, autism."

I related to everything he said, because it's my life and I'm living through it, too. It's funny, we live in the same house, with the same children and the same problems, but we deal with things in completely different ways.

I often wonder if he struggles more than I do, because he's away so much for work. I used to question why he'd come home miserable or unhappy, because he's just had a break from all this. But when I see it from his perspective, he's been in London having a great time, and to come back to a difficult environment, it must be hard. It's just been part of our life and our journey, and for me, we just need to do something good with it.

My husband also explained in that interview that he believes there is an autistic spectrum. At the moment, there's a huge debate about it. For example, our Leo has the highest score on the spectrum. He ticks more boxes and has more autistic traits than the girls, but then some of his symptoms are milder than theirs.

Just because the girls have a lower score on the spectrum

and tick less boxes, it doesn't make them any easier and they can be just as difficult. They're all considered moderately autistic in medical terms, and it just depends on how their day's going and what's triggered them off as to how severe their condition can be. Sometimes they can have a great day, others not so. There are days where any of my children could seem severely autistic, and there are others when you wouldn't even know they're autistic at all.

So, there is an argument at the moment over whether the spectrum should exist, and that's exactly why – because your rating on the scale is about how many boxes you tick; not how severe you are overall. But I don't focus on it. I don't think about where they fall on the spectrum, I just take everything as it comes.

Each day is different, but what I will say is that it is rare that all three of them will have a 'normal day'. There'll always be something. But it keeps me busy and continuously learning.

One of the things my husband and I are discussing quite a lot is how autistic people are not really considered for jobs, relationships or friendships.

They're maybe seen as a bit of a hindrance, quite particular or difficult. It's such a huge spectrum, that unless you've got autism in your family, I can see why you'd struggle to understand it.

But there are definitely stereotypes around autism. And when people hear the word 'autistic', they assume the worst straight away. Autistic people are quite often written off and not seen for all the amazing qualities that they do have.

And unfortunately, prejudice does exist.

As well as that rude person asking me if I wished I'd never had children, there was another instance where we had a problem with my blue parking badge.

To be honest, I rarely use it, but I have it because of the sheer volume of hospital appointments I go to with my children. The kids have no awareness of danger and sometimes they do run off, which is worrying if we're in a busy car park.

And because of Leo's hypermobility, there is that physical side of requiring it, too.

On this day, I was going to the gym. I was taking the children to the crèche there and parked in a disabled space, because it was really close to the door and I was on my own with all three children.

A man approached me.

"Why are you parked there?" he shouted aggressively.

"You're not disabled. There's nothing wrong with you!"

Because I was in front of the kids, I quietly replied, "It's actually my children. All three of them are autistic." I tried to explain it to him, but he was having none of it. He refused to believe it was OK for us to leave the car in a disabled space.

Deeply upset, I took the children to the crèche and didn't bother going to the gym to work out.

I made my way to the café and had a cup of tea while I thought it all over. I informed the leisure centre staff about it, too. It was a really emotional day for me.

A couple of weeks later, I went back to the gym and the staff told me the said man had gone away and done his research about autism. He wanted to apologise for shouting and questioning everything.

It's just a shame. Whether you can see someone's disability or not, if that individual has a blue badge, don't interrogate them. You don't know what that person's going through.

He could have really affected my children's behaviour that day and put us in a very dangerous position. Most of the time, I don't go anywhere with all three children on my own, because of how unsafe it can be. They have no sense of risk and are far from streetwise.

But to take the beautiful from this nightmare, that day taught someone something. He went away, looked it up and apologised.

I think the image of the blue badge needs to change as it's outdated. A picture of a person in a wheelchair isn't a true reflection of all people with disabilities. It's a symbol that's recognised globally, so sadly it's not something that's going to be replaced overnight, but I do believe people's attitudes need to change.

Another instance of discrimination was when I was looking into potential schools for the twins. I went to visit

12 schools before I chose the amazing primary the children attend now.

At the time I didn't know the twins were autistic, but because of their speech delay, I knew there was something going on. So, I told a teacher at one of the schools I was visiting about it.

"They're doing really well. They're non-verbal, but they're having speech and language therapy and they'll probably come along with some support," I explained.

This lady obviously saw a red flag straight away. She probably knew the twins were autistic before I did.

"OK, and do you think this school will be able to support your children?" she asked.

A bit stunned, I bumbled, "Well, I really like the school. We only live five minutes away…"

"I've still got some schools to visit, but I'll get back in touch," I told her, before walking off.

Within a couple of days, I had an email from the school telling me there weren't any places left.

It never said so in the email, but I know it's because my children need extra support. They did have places. It was a private school that was happy to take anyone's money. But not mine.

She was more than comfortable to show me around, but as soon as she found out there were some additional needs there with the twins, they suddenly didn't have any space. It's disgusting, and at the time it really upset me. But now

I think, *thank God.* I would not want my children to go to a school that's not fully inclusive, that doesn't accept children with hidden disabilities and wouldn't provide them with the support they need. It was a blessing that they were rejected, really.

But this all happened at the beginning of their autism journey and I just thought, *are they going to get turned away forever?*

It's been a constant battle of being left out and treated differently. We'd see our friends having BBQs with their friends and their children and we wouldn't get invited. And I remember thinking, *it's because my kids are autistic.*

Thinking about it, whoever organised it was probably aware it would be difficult and upsetting for us, as things would usually end up in tears.

We do avoid a lot of family parties, because the children struggle with it. It's difficult because they are starting to be invited to a lot of parties. Luckily, they've got a close group of friends, and a lot of them are autistic as well, so I suppose all us mums understand each other.

It's been difficult to get to this point, but they are doing amazingly and managing to do more activities. I wish everyone understood it a little bit better. I hope by the time they're teenagers we'll live in a much more understanding and inclusive society.

And it's true some people have got such a bad perception of autism because of what they've seen in the press. All they've heard is how difficult it is – and it is. Believe me, I'm not trying to sugar coat it, things can be really challenging. But on the other side of the coin, we are lucky because we get to celebrate so much more, and the little milestones they've achieved. For example, the first time they walked on the beach, or boarded a plane, or said "I love you". All of these things that people take for granted, we've been able to draw great joy from.

It's a hard road to acceptance. Some parents aren't sure if they want our children to hang around with theirs, because they think they're going to pick up some bad traits. I can only speak for my children, but they are able to communicate and socialise. It is difficult for them, but they can do it and deserve a chance as much as anyone.

I still find it madness how they're not included more – especially adults going for jobs. At the moment, the National Autistic Society is reporting that only 22% of autistic people are in work. That's madness. I'm really hoping this will change.

If they're capable of doing something, allow them to do it. They are capable of doing things. There are companies now that will actually only employ autistic people, which is brilliant, because they know if they've got a passion or focus for something, they could probably do something ten times better than what we could.

Slowly, people are catching on that they can be quite a credit. It will be autistic people that cure cancer and invent new technologies, like Microsoft and Apple. There will be people working in those businesses with autism. I've got my own three little geniuses at home.

I do hope Leo, Penelope and Felicity will be independent one day. Realistically, I don't think they'll be completely self-sufficient, but I believe that they'll need minimal support when they're adults. If we keep giving them the help and support that they need now, I think they'll get a job and be able to drive.

I don't know if they'll have relationships, but if they do and they're happy then that's great. I know they're so capable, and I wouldn't want to write them off before they've tried anything.

A constant argument between me and my husband is him thinking they're not going to be able to do anything and I'm constantly saying they will.

What I'm seeing at the minute is more and more autistic adults in workplaces, which is amazing. You see them with their Sunflower lanyards on, and I recognise it.

I was talking to a lady a couple of weeks ago as she was working in the shop. She started talking to me about autism and said, "I'm just like your children." She had her lanyard on, so I knew. She said her mum was told the same – that she would never speak, or drive. But she's doing all these things now.

You can tell she needs a little bit of support, but she's driving, she's in a relationship and she works in a shop. I just thought, *if my children are doing that as adults, I'll be so proud and happy.*

And all the hard work I've put in for years, taking them to appointments and different therapies, is really paying off. I feel so upbeat about my children's future.

My husband and I are also trying to use our platform in a really positive way, to help change people's perceptions.

While writing my book, we're filming the BBC documentary, which we hope will make a difference in breaking the stigma. And our aim is to show people there have been so many great things to take from our experience as parents to autistic children.

People often ask how I cope with it all and what I always say is, I just don't know any different. I've always been a mum to children with additional needs and in many ways, it's made me a stronger and a better person. And I appreciate everything I have.

It's also taught me a patience I never knew I had.

Because of everything I've dealt with, with the children, I do feel quite invincible. Like there's nothing in life that can hit me harder than that.

13

A Day In The Life

My day-to-day life is really full-on, and everything I do is carefully planned around the children. The reality is I don't have a lot of time for myself, so every moment is precious. I wouldn't change it for the world, though.

I always wake up having had very little sleep, because of my insomnia struggles.

Felicity is also like her mummy and not a good sleeper, and it's not unusual for her to wake every hour.

Penelope is always the first up and rises around 5am.

I'll spend the first couple of hours getting her ready, then Leo wakes around 7am.

Then, I repeat the cycle with him and Felicity. They can't dress themselves yet, but I don't mind helping. Next, there's the task of getting all three of them out the door.

I'll drive them to school. There used to be two drop-offs – the twins to school and Felicity to nursery – but now she's started primary it's just one commute in the morning.

Once home, I'll get myself showered, dressed and ready. There's just no way I can do this before the school run.

And that will leave me with a couple of hours to get work done, clean, and get the washing machine going. Then there's things like food shopping and other everyday mundane things. There's no glamour here!

If I've got any free time, then I'll go to the gym. And once a month, I'll treat myself to a hair wash and blow-dry at the salon.

Before I know it, it's time to collect the children. As soon as we're home, I'll put the kids in their pyjamas and sort their tea out. Bedtime can be a bit all over the place, but I try to stick to a routine. It'll usually be dinner, bath and storytime. We have a story every single night, which the kids love and I do too.

The twins will settle down for bed around 9.30pm, while Felicity can be a livewire and will be running around upstairs screaming and shouting, sometimes until 2am.

She's not being naughty, she's just really excited to be awake. It's just me and her a lot of the time during those early hours. I'm hoping she'll calm down, because Leo used to really struggle to go to sleep, too. When he was four, I had to push him in a pram to get him to sleep, but now he's older, he's better with it.

So, this is my day-to-day routine, but I'm trying to schedule some 'me time' as well a couple of times a month. Whether that be work, or socialising with friends.

I just need to try to keep some routine for the kids there, so it's normal for me to go away, because they started getting really clingy again after the lockdowns.

Going away is getting easier, and the mum guilt is easing off a bit now. But it's something I destroyed myself with for years, leaving them at home and feeling rubbish about it.

I even worried about sharing my outings on social media, if I was working. I'd always have that fear of being judged. Sadly, it's one of those inequalities between men and women.

Mums always get asked, "Where are your kids?" Whereas my husband can be away for weeks and no one will question it.

I'm at the point now where I'm thinking, *this is really good for me, for them and for my husband*. I'm trying to fit it in where possible, but it depends when Patrick's working.

Our lives are really normal – just two parents juggling work with family life.

ƒMy husband is one of the biggest TV hosts in the UK, so the perception is that it's all red carpets and the clinking of champagne glasses. But in reality, our life is so average. It's just Mum and Dad at home.

Our house might be a bit bigger and our cars might be a bit nicer than what we had growing up, but the family values are still there. We want to be parents who spend quality time at home with the kiddies, and we're just trying to get through each day.

Don't get me wrong, it's exhausting, but I wouldn't change it.

14

Back To School

As well as our already hectic schedules, one of the constants that's been around since the children were little is their appointments.

We're used to making the trip to the hospital on a regular basis, it's become second nature for us, and above all we're so grateful that this help is available for our children.

Speech and language therapy is one of the first sessions the children had and it's still ongoing now. That's been the most consistent treatment.

When you start going to the appointments it's just about getting the children playing. At the beginning of the journey, I was sitting there thinking, *how is this going to help teach my children to talk?* But it works and it really has made such an improvement in their speech.

The therapists know what they're doing and I'm so pleased this is available on the NHS for parents like myself, unsure on what to do.

The twins still have speech and language therapy now in school, and it's just become a part of life for them. It suddenly doesn't feel like a hospital appointment anymore and they actually get excited to go and play with the toys. While they're playing, the therapists will be asking them questions, to prompt them to speak. They won't just assess how they pronounce the words, a lot of it is about the answers they provide.

It's been really interesting. I've learnt a lot about it myself, and I'm lucky to be able to carry it on at home. These appointments are getting less, which is a good thing, because it means the children are doing better without the extra support.

Leo has occupational therapy for his hypermobility. It's quite common for children with autism to have a double-barrelled diagnosis with something else, which can come on in their childhood and teenage years.

At first it was every few weeks, and then when he started school the therapist went into his class and taught Leo's one-to-one what to do with him, so that he could have it there. That was ideal, because they didn't want to have to keep disturbing his school routine. It's basically little exercises to help his ligaments and joints.

If he gets better with his diet, his hypermobility should

improve as he gets bigger and stronger. And building muscle can really help, but he's too young for that now.

It's just to make the area around his joints and ligaments a bit more solid, because at the moment he's like an elastic band. It's not uncommon for gymnasts at the Olympics to have hypermobility, so it's not necessarily a bad thing. It's just something we keep an eye on.

He has eye check-ups every six weeks, because of his short-sightedness. He's really good and wears his glasses all the time. It used to be awful going to the appointments all the time with him, but thankfully he's used to it now.

Food play therapy is for Leo, as although the girls have difficulty with eating too, they eat more than he does.

In the appointments, they do things like putting cereal in a tray and then running toy tractors through it, crunching it and saying, "Listen to the sound, Leo." And I'd be thinking, *you can't eat that, it's all dirty*. Although I understand now, the food play was never about making him eat, it was getting him comfortable with it.

We went for months playing with dry food, and then eventually she'd pour a bit of water in there, so it would be wet. Then she'd put a bit of paint in there, and he would touch that. It took years and years of this therapy, but now he touches the wet food. It was about breaking down the barriers and getting over the sensory stuff.

That's actually something I struggle with myself. If there's play slime anywhere in the house, I can't touch it!

Even feeding the cat has become a problem, because of the smell of the cat food and the thought of it touching my hand makes me want to vomit.

Leo still has appointments with the nutritionist and that's the most upsetting one for me, because of the eating disorder I suffered with for years.

I don't actually think he feels hungry, and the milkshakes we found for him were a blessing. I'd rather see him eating a burger, than having a shake, but it means we avoid him having that PEG operation.

It's awful seeing your child getting that poorly. The appointments feel like they have been going on forever, but it's getting better because they have been taken over by the school.

The most difficult time I had with these sessions was when I was taking Leo and Penelope to the hospital regularly while I was heavily pregnant with Felicity. That was exhausting. Then, I had to do it with Felicity when she was a newborn. So, it was a relief when their routine check-ups got moved over to the school. I'm trying to see it as a positive, but it's quite scary when they've relied on help and you've seen how much it's supported them in their development.

It's a good thing that their appointments are reducing, because they don't need them as much, and that's what we want. We want them to be independent. We're trying to cut them down at school too, because we don't want them to be secluded from the rest of the class. It's probably me struggling more than them with the thought of everything.

The concept of them being on their own at school is petrifying, but that's my worries more than anything else.

Speaking of school, while working on my book, Felicity had her first day at the same primary the twins go to and while she did so well, it turned out to be a nightmare – of course!

We'd been thoroughly preparing for this day. Felicity visited the school beforehand and then over the summer holidays we tried to keep her routine the same as it was, so she carried on doing her normal hours at nursery up until the point she started school in September.

Her new teacher even went to visit her while she was at nursery and got to know Felicity and her mannerisms. The teacher spoke to the nursery staff and got to understand her little ways – what she likes and what she doesn't like – and she asked her about food. Felicity's a bit better with her eating than Leo, but everything is still beige. If she's going to have pasta for example, it won't have sauce smothered over it.

The nursery have helpfully passed that information onto the school, so it made it that bit easier when Felicity did eventually make the move. And, despite my initial nervousness, she got through her first full day of school without any hiccups.

I've seen such a change in her already. On the first night,

she went to bed at 9.30pm. And while that's still late for a five-year-old, it's amazing for Felicity.

I went into her bedroom, just thinking I'd try my luck, and said, "Felicity, now you're at big school, we need to turn your television off and we have to go night nights. OK?"

And she said, "OK, Mummy. I love you, night night." I kind of stood there for a minute, thinking, *what has changed in this child?!* She slept over eight hours and part of me thought, *has she been able to do that for five years and just had me pissing about every night?*

She already seems to be more grown-up. I'm not sure how long it will last, though.

I've been trying to get her into bed earlier for ages. A few days before the first school day, I said to her, "Come on, we need to start going to sleep now. I don't want you being tired at big school."

"But Mummy, I don't know how to go to sleep," she replied.

And I really felt for her, because I'm the same. I sometimes lay there at night looking at Patrick and thinking, *how do you do that?*

I must sleep at some point, but I don't know how he does it. He literally just puts his head on the pillow and goes to sleep.

But while Felicity's first day was a success overall, it wasn't without its dramas.

On the Monday morning, I had them all ready to go.

Penelope was feeling a bit worried because she really panics about being late for school, which I understand as I used to be like that.

She really does feel that anxiety if we're going anywhere, but school especially.

All morning she was saying, "Mum, we're going to be late."

"No, we are not! We're going to be there on time," I reassured her. I was determined.

It's funny because Penelope is like a sergeant major in the mornings.

"Did you get my pencil case? My pen? Did you get my blazer? Have you got my water?" she kept reminding me.

She wanted to make sure she had everything – I think it's because she's scared of getting in trouble.

Anyway, I was driving from the house, and I was only minutes away from home when the car swerved. I could feel something wasn't right with the wheel and there was no one around, because it was really early morning. I carried on driving really slowly and it kept pulling and pulling to one side, so I just said to the kids, "Mummy just needs to stop for one minute."

I pulled over and straight away Penelope's screaming in the back of the car.

"Are we going to die, Mummy?" she asked me, in a really posh voice. Sometimes Penelope's reactions seem really dramatic and that's because a typical autistic trait is masking. For example, if she has seen a similar situation in a film, she will imitate it, even if the situation isn't as bad.

I was like, "No, it's fine. I just need to check the car."

I've never been on time for anything in my life, and I was determined to be punctual, but things never seem to go quite to plan. While I was checking this flat tyre, Penelope was having a panic attack in the back of the car. Then, Leo started screaming. So, I had to get back in the vehicle.

"Listen, Mummy's going to drive home really slowly," I reassured them.

That got Penelope even more worked up, and she said, "We can't go home, it's the first day of school." And then Felicity started, too.

I don't know how I've managed to laugh about it, but if our day didn't go wrong, it wouldn't be right.

I had to drive home really carefully and luckily Patrick was working that day, and he'd gone with a chauffeur, so his car was still parked on the drive.

I was able to get home safely, get the children out of the car, pop them in a different car and then drive off to school. But we were 40 minutes late.

When we eventually arrived at the school gates, all the children started walking past the car with their blazers on, going to assembly. And a distressed Penelope was shouting, "They're leaving without us!"

"They're all early," I fibbed.

Such a little thing like that, a bloody puncture or

whatever it was, set my poor Penelope up for the worst day ever.

So, dropping them off on the first day of school didn't quite go to plan. But I spoke to Penelope's one-to-one and warned her, "Listen, she's all worked up and she's going to be anxious now."

The other two were also on edge – it's like a domino effect with my children. The staff had a bit of time with them on their own and they texted me later on saying, "Just to let you know, they're OK. They're nice and calm, and they're having a good day."

And that was it. When I went to pick them up, it was lovely getting all three of them from one place.

But I will miss going to nursery, because I'd been going there for years with the twins and then Felicity. It's weird to think I'm not going to pop in there again.

The staff sort of became friends, because they'd been there through everything – the children's diagnoses, tears every now and then… And they learnt so much from our children, so I've got to know them really well.

But they're all in full-time education and that's an achievement in itself, because we didn't know if that was something that was going to happen.

I nearly burst with pride when I saw Felicity chatting to another child, which for her is quite a big deal.

She can be so vocal, where she's the loudest in the room, but sometimes she can be so shy that she won't speak.

It's great she's gone straight in, full of personality and absolutely amazed me. That's one of the good things with our children, they continue to surprise us. I never underestimate them anyway, I think they're capable of anything.

But there's always that little seed of doubt there in my head – is their autism going to hold them back? But they're doing absolutely amazing, and I can't believe what they're accomplishing. All three of my babies are now in school, how incredible!

It's funny when I look back, the twins' first day at school was completely different to Felicity's.

Obviously, this time round with the car disaster there wasn't time to worry. I was too stressed thinking, *right, I've dropped her off, I've got five hours to get some work done, have a shower and wash my hair*. I went to the gym for a little bit to de-stress and I sorted my tyre out. My day was full to the brim. Whereas when the twins went to school for the first time the worries were different. They were nowhere near as verbal as Felicity, and they weren't using the toilet on their own.

I knew they weren't going to eat there, and they didn't. Whereas with Felicity, I was kind of hoping that she would, but I wasn't sure. Just in case, I put a little packed lunch in her bag – and to my amazement, she ate her ham sandwich!

I feel like we were more prepared with Felicity, and the school was too. And because we can talk to her about it, because she can speak more confidently than the twins did at that age, she knew what was happening. She understood it. With the twins, it felt like the longest day in the world. I sat at home crying and had the school on speed dial.

It was completely different and I really believe it's because it was down to early intervention. We knew what to do. Like with any situation, if you know what to do it becomes easier.

It's early days, and I think it will hit her that she's not going back to nursery and she's not going to see those children again.

Especially one of her friends, which she's had throughout. I don't think she's realised she's not going to be around the other children she's used to. But she seems happy and keeps telling me she's a big girl now and is filling me in on all the rules, like wearing a blazer every day and reading a story.

She's still trying to understand it and it will take a while for her to get her head around school life. For example, I said to her, "What lessons did you do today?"

"Oh, I don't have lessons!" she replied.

"Did you do numbers? Did you do some reading?"

"Oh yes, we read stories."

"Well, that's a lesson."

Academically, she's excelling, like the twins, and they're really intelligent children, but the little things that most kids would know – that a lesson is called a lesson – she struggles to understand.

I still believe she's going to surpass our expectations – they all will!

Patrick and I are so thankful that we've managed to navigate this crazy celebrity world and raise three beautiful children, but it's not been without its challenges.

15

If You've Got Laughter, You've Got Everything

I knew from the beginning I was never going to leave him. Right from when I first saw the photos, I knew it wasn't the end.

We'd been through lots of difficult times in our marriage, but this was the first time it became public.

It all unravelled on February 11, 2018. I woke up early in the morning. Felicity, who was one at the time, was in the cot next to me and the twins were in bed asleep.

Patrick had spent weeks in London. He was filming The Keith & Paddy Picture Show and was due to come back, but rang me to tell me he was exhausted.

"Stay down there," I told him, calmly.

"Get your work done and come home when you're ready."

He'd been filming the show for months and I knew he was struggling with life at home – the sleepless nights, the children being non-verbal and barely eating – so he would often stay away for a bit of a break. And I was fine with it. So, with my encouragement, he stopped over in London for the weekend.

Little did I know the drama that would unfold.

As I roused from sleep that Sunday morning, I looked down at my phone and saw some alerts had come up and a couple of text messages.

"Hope you're OK," my manager at the time texted me. "Give me a ring whenever you're ready. I'm here!"

I clicked onto Instagram, where I'd been tagged in some posts. Then I saw them – pictures and videos of my husband and another woman out in London. And they were everywhere.

My husband, arm-in-arm with another woman. I felt physically sick. I ran to the toilet to vomit. Still to this day I can remember that absolutely awful pit-of-your-stomach feeling.

My mum was staying with us that weekend, like she did quite often, and was sleeping on the top floor when I discovered the images.

I phoned her from my bed.

"What's happened? Are you OK?" she answered.

She came down to our bedroom and I showed her everything. Needless to say, she was absolutely devastated and heartbroken for me.

"I don't want to be here when he comes back, but I don't want to leave you on your own," she confessed.

At this point I still hadn't spoken to him, so I wasn't sure if he was even coming back or what was going on.

I rang him that morning before I'd read too much about it. I'd only seen a couple of pictures at this point. He didn't answer, which is really unusual for him and in hindsight I think he massively regrets not picking up the phone. It quickly dawned on me the reason he'd decided to stay down in London and that prompted me to post a quote on Instagram.

"I believe everything happens for a reason," it said. "People change so you can learn to let go, things go wrong so that you can appreciate them when they're right.

"You believe lies so that you will eventually learn to trust no one but yourself, and sometimes good things fall apart so better things can fall together."

"When you realise you deserve so much more... that's not a bad thing," I also tweeted.

It was a bit of a heartbroken moment.

I was absolutely devastated by these pictures of my husband with another woman.

I'd never been the jealous type. I had seen a few exchanges between Patrick and the other woman on social media, but thought nothing of it, Patrick has a lot of female friends in the industry.

After my social media posts, my phone started blowing up. I had loads of messages from people saying, "I hope you sort it out."

"Leave him. Don't stay with him," others told me.

In the space of a few hours, suddenly everyone had an opinion on my marriage, and I didn't know what was going on myself!

My husband was aware he'd been videoed by someone, as he asked them to stop filming when he was walking down the street with the other woman.

But I still don't know if he was warned or not about the images being leaked to the press, but I don't believe he was.

Patrick eventually phoned me back in the afternoon. I didn't answer. He kept ringing and ringing, and I refused to pick up. I totally ignored him. I was too upset.

He wasn't supposed to be coming home that night, he was due to carry on filming with Leigh, but he rushed back from London.

"I'm coming home. I'm coming back, please speak to me," he urged over text message. I didn't reply.

Throughout his four-hour journey home to Cheshire, he carried on texting me.

"I'm two hours away," another message came through.

I broke the news to my mum that he was going to be arriving soon.

"I'm going to go," she told me. "I don't want to be here. I don't want to look at him!"

It was nighttime, the children were in bed and I was waiting alone for my husband to return. My husband who had been pictured arm-in-arm with another woman for all the world to see.

He eventually arrived. I have to say we really didn't speak much about it. There were no rows or arguments, but I just didn't want to look at him.

He was at home for two days before he returned to London for work. While he carried on filming, my life in Cheshire became a nightmare.

The story continued to garner attention and suddenly everyone was interested in what I was doing and what was going on.

Journalists rang the doorbell to my house all day and all night. They were knocking on my mum's door, too. I'd have photographers following me while I was doing the school run.

I tried to carry on with my life. I wasn't in the limelight or in the media at all up until this point, and just like that I was being hounded.

The showbiz stuff was my husband's side of work, and I was just a stay-at-home mum. I felt like I was thrown into the tabloid world and not in a way I wanted. It was like a horrible whirlwind that took over our lives, but I couldn't split up with him at this point, I just couldn't.

My worry, more than anything, was − is it affecting the children? I couldn't go anywhere without being followed. This went on for about six weeks after the pictures came out.

I remember one of the first times I left the house, when my marriage was splashed across the newspapers, was to go to the hairdressers.

I didn't realise how big that story was, because I don't really read papers or magazines, or even Google myself. I'd had the appointment booked for weeks and I just thought, *no, I haven't done anything wrong, I'm going to carry on with my life and go and get my hair done.*

I was in the salon for a couple of hours before suddenly somebody said, "There's a photographer outside the window."

Then there was another one, and another. I was in there for a while, and by the end of the appointment there were around ten photographers waiting for me that I had to walk out to on my own. That's when it hit me how massive the story was.

After being blinded by cameras flashing, I got in the car and cried my eyes out − you may have seen the pictures! I broke down before I drove home. It suddenly felt really real that people knew what was going on in my marriage.

I didn't go out much after that. Although, one day after dropping the kids off at school and nursery, I couldn't face returning to our marital home, so I drove to Blackpool. I don't often go and see my family there, as you know we're not close, but I try to visit at least once a year.

I walked into my nan and grandad's house and to my surprise, sitting there, was my dad.

It was the healthiest I'd ever seen him in my life. He'd come off the heroin for a bit and was having methadone from the pharmacy. It's probably one of the few times in my life where I really needed my dad. And he just held me while I cried my eyes out. At that point in time, I was so glad to have my father there.

I still have a really nice photo from that day, where he looks so well and I look bloody awful.

It just felt so nice to have a normal cup of tea with my dad and grandparents. Nan had been with my grandad since they were teenagers and they were still married up until the day he died, last year.

"Marriage is difficult, I've been through it all with Grandad and look at us now," she told me. "I wouldn't be without him."

That advice has always stuck with me. People go through difficult times in marriage, family, work, life – everything. Everyone has tough periods, but you've just got to get through it. Stick together if you can, if not go your separate ways.

But for me, I wanted my children to have a dad at home. It didn't matter to me if I'd forgiven him, if I was OK with it or if I trusted him. All of that didn't count, I just wanted my children to have their father there – something I never had.

For that to happen, I had to brush it under the carpet. So, that's what I did and I haven't mentioned it since. We've never spoken about it really, and I've certainly never talked about it publicly before.

While this was all going on, my 30th birthday was looming. It was a birthday I'll never forget, but not the celebrations I'd hoped for.

Just before my marriage hit this incredibly difficult time, I was in talks with The Real Housewives Of Cheshire producers to join as a guest Housewife.

I'd been approached on many occasions over the years to be a part of the show and always turned them down, because I just didn't have the time.

But this was a period in my life when I really wanted to do something for me. I needed to get out of the house and mix with other people, and in a way, I suppose a bit of respite from all the challenges I was facing every day at home.

Although I still couldn't commit to becoming a full-time cast member, the producers agreed I could join as a guest Housewife and they would work around my schedule.

But let's just say it didn't go down well at home. Patrick didn't want me to have a public profile at all. He especially didn't want me to join this show. He thought it was all about the glitz and glamour, and showing off your wealth, which is so far-removed from my normal life. And I agree it wasn't quite the right fit; I don't live a glamorous life and I'm not shopping for Chanel bags and going to swanky parties every day, which is the reputation of Housewives.

But it was a chance to do *something!* It was local to where I lived and a chance for me to make friends and have some sort of a social and work life, which had been non-existent in my twenties. And, most importantly, I could fit it in around the children, just a couple of hours filming here and there. So, I said yes. Being a part of the show was great fun and I enjoyed the experience I had, but it's just not my real life.

Anyway, during the midst of filming, the producers invited me on a girls' trip to Morocco. This was just weeks after my marriage struggles had been plastered all over the internet and newspapers for the whole world to see.

Most of the other cast members went for a week, but I agreed to fly over for a couple of days to join them.

The day I left was my 30th birthday – and no one knew it was. I boarded the plane alone and cried my eyes out the whole journey, thinking about how awful things were.

So, yeah, not the way I thought I'd be celebrating the big 3-0.

I was so tiny, too. I'd dropped an incredible amount of weight in about two weeks, and my clothes were hanging off me.

But I must admit, as much as it was a stressful time filming Housewives in Marrakech, it was a really good distraction. And as much as my husband hated it and didn't want me to be involved with the show, he should be really grateful for it, because it made me not focus on what was going on at home.

For the whole of my twenties, I stayed in. I cooked, cleaned and looked after our children. It obviously didn't work for our marriage anyway, so I thought, I may as well go and do what I want to do. I always wanted to work. For me it was never about being a 'celebrity'. I just wanted to be out there, earning. Where I was raised, nobody really had much and I always had that fire in my belly where I wanted to do something. I'd done everything he wanted for so long and turned down jobs and TV work, and I got to the point where I thought, *I want to do stuff and be happy, too*. I wanted my children to grow up and see Mummy works as well as Daddy. I'm still so glad I did it.

Time rumbled on and eventually the newspapers stopped printing the pictures and writing about what they thought was going on in our marriage. We never separated and that's something that was inaccurately reported in the press. There were stories saying I'd kicked him out – I never did or would ever do that. No matter how difficult things get, I would never kick my husband out. We said nothing and within a couple of weeks we were out and about as though nothing ever happened. We just got on with married life. I'm glad we did, because his bond with the children is so much better than it ever was then. And he makes so much

Left: Working out with one of my closest friends Nelly

Above: I wore this insane gown and tiara for my Real Housewives Of Cheshire debut at the Decadence Ball

Left: A bit more gym time!

Above left: Back in 2007, this man (Dave), introduced me to my future husband! Above right: I was honoured to be the first mum ever to front an Ann Summers campaign. Below left: I had some wild experiences while filming Housewives – including this visit to a fetish party with my best friend Adam! Below right: Attending the BRIT Awards with Patrick in 2011. It was our first time on the red carpet together

Above: Being photographed in public became part of everyday life
Below: Me and my bump! I was nine months pregnant with Felicity here

Above: At the National Diversity Awards in Liverpool's Anglican Cathedral this year. I was nominated for an award for my campaigning around autism

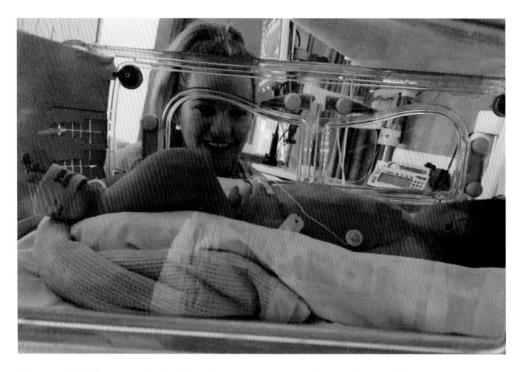

Above: Felicity needed a bit of extra support when she was born. It was such a scary time

Below left: Using a visual calendar makes life so much easier

Below right: Paddy and Leo having fun in the sand on our first family holiday to Mallorca. This was a huge milestone for my children

Left: Having twins has always kept me on my toes

Above: Playing with toys is a different experience for my children

Below: Seeing red. My kiddies are all big Liverpool fans (of course!) and love wearing the kit of their favourite team

Below: The children chose their own mismatched clothing and hairstyles on this day. I chose not to have a battle about it!

Above: The pictures on our clock help the kids make sense of the time

Below: The McGuinness clan on a family day out. I've been careful about protecting my kiddies' identity on social media

Above: I'll do anything to help my kids – even bake pastry letters! **Right:** All three of my children are now at primary school. Where has the time gone?

Left: In Cambridge on the day I received my autism diagnosis

Left: Attending the 2019 Pride Of Britain Awards.
I love hearing the many inspirational stories

Below: I'm so proud of being an ambassador for the National Autistic Society

We recently celebrated our 10th anniversary!

more of an effort to be at home as much as possible. Instead of staying over in London when he's filming, he'll actually drive through the night back to Cheshire, so he can be with us all in the morning.

As much as our time apart helps us, because it is full-on, I think he needed to be at home to bond with the children properly. He needed to see how much I was doing, too.

It's been incredible, because I've seen such a difference in him as a husband and father since that difficult patch. He's made changes in himself without me asking him to.

The children have their daddy at home, which is all I ever wanted, and I still have my husband at home, which is what I want – I married for life.

I hope and believe our marriage is really good and we are happy. Of course there are times when things are difficult and we can't stand each other, but the majority of the time, we laugh and joke and we're getting on with life as a little team.

It's a happy home, not a volatile home, and we never argue. That's just not my style. Even at the most difficult time in our marriage, we didn't row, argue or shout. I'm a laid-back, open-minded person and I knew I didn't want to lose my husband. We've got to be united for our kids.

Looking back, I think things became difficult when the children were so young. You're up in the night, you're tired and trying to work when you haven't had any sleep. There was the added stress of having a hospital appointment every other day, the children weren't speaking or eating and he really struggled with their autism diagnoses. I think it's fair to say he found working away easier than life was at home. It's hard, but if you can ride out those first couple of years where it's horrendous, your life does come back and I hope now Felicity has started school, Patrick and I will be able to spend a bit more time together during the day.

We're very lucky, and we both agree, as testing as things get, we laugh, and if you've got laughter, you've got everything. That's what Peter Kay said to us on our wedding day, and it's so true.

We find laughter in everything, and I love laughing. That's why I made the right choice in marrying a comedian.

16

All That Glitters

I joined the cast of The Real Housewives Of Cheshire in 2018, amid a difficult time in my marriage. And even though I'm no longer on the show, and it was the right decision to leave when I did, I'm so grateful for the freedom it gave me.

At the time of joining the series, I felt scared and alone, but I just had to push myself to get out of the house. I was absolutely determined to do something.

Although filming was right on my doorstep, socialising felt like foreign territory for me, because throughout my twenties all I did was isolate myself at home. During that time, I went to a couple of red-carpet events, but I was quite reclusive and my confidence was on the floor.

I had zero social skills, probably because I didn't go to school for most of my teenage years.

A Beautiful Nightmare

On the odd occasion Patrick and I would go to a charity event together, we'd walk into the room and everyone would stop to speak to him and I would be sat, thinking, *please, no one talk to me, I've got nothing to say.*

I'd make excuses all the time. If he was busy chatting with people, I'd go and hide in the toilet just to get out of the room.

It's funny, Patrick and I were talking recently about an outing to the BRIT Awards in 2011, and we look back at that night completely differently.

We'd been together four years and it was one of the few and first red carpets I attended with him. He was reminiscing about how we managed to blag a boat across the Thames and that's what he remembers about that night. But my vivid recollection of that evening was making myself sick on the train down to London.

I was panicking about my gown. My little black dress was a size 0 and still it was too big. It's mad because he doesn't remember it like this at all. I was so stressed about the wedding at the time and I was just skin and bone. Everyone said, "You look so amazing." But I was so weak I could barely stand up, it was awful and I'd never want to go back to that. That was probably my tiniest time as an adult. I was only around seven stone.

For me, that was an awful evening and I barely left the house much after that. But life was completely different for Patrick. For the first five years of having the kids, he carried on having his holidays and golfing trips. I never did, and I didn't have friends to go away with anyway. But I'd always wave him off and say, "Go and enjoy yourself, have a lovely time."

Secretly, I'd resent him so much. He'd come back with the best tan ever and I'd be exhausted after having the children on my own for that time. I'd think, *God, I wish I could do that and have a little weekend getaway.*

I wanted that freedom so much, but I just didn't have it.

I struggled with the whole life he was living, because it was not my life, it was his. I was just a wife at home and he had this completely different, separate existence I wasn't part of. Then when we went through that difficult time in our marriage, that kicked me up the arse to get out and do something that was my own. And follow my own dreams.

Even the dancing and modelling I did years ago was all a part of me desperately trying to better myself and to do something for my life and have some independence. I lost that during my twenties, when I was trying to be a good wife and mum.

And although there was no denying I needed some sort of break, no one close to me really wanted me to become a Cheshire Housewife, least of all my husband. He didn't want a wife in the public eye, and this show's reputation was that of drama and glitzy parties. Neither of which was or is now my life. I was just a full-time mother to our children.

Patrick wasn't the only one against me doing the show –

my mum had her concerns, too. She worried I would come across as a stereotypical Cheshire Housewife, which I'm not.

Not everyone understood my reasons for wanting to do it, and you feel shit having to explain yourself – especially when it was quite a nervous period anyway. I was leaving the children for the first time ever, going on telly and opening myself up to public opinion. It was a lot to think about. It's not an easy decision to be in the limelight, but I kind of already was by default.

So, after breaking the news to my loved ones, it was now down to the job at hand – filming. My first day on set was a memorable one.

The only Housewife I really knew was Tanya Bardsley. We'd met on a photoshoot years before, and we'd both been pregnant at the same time.

She's a really lovely person, and we're still friends now. I'd obviously seen the other girls out and about in Cheshire, but Tanya was the Housewife I was the closest with.

We filmed my debut in a shopping centre in Manchester, and I had to just 'bump into' the girls.

My instruction was to not-so-subtly walk past Tanya and Ester Dee and wait for them to clock me.

Obviously, I knew Tanya before, but I'd never met Ester. I had to stroll into the shot where they were filming, and they weren't aware I was coming.

"Oh my God, Christine!" Tanya shrieked immediately, which put me at ease.

It then got awkward because the ladies had to react as though we're not on camera, and straight away, Ester being Ester, went, "Oh my God, are you the new Housewife?!"

So, we had to do it again. The three of us giggled and Ester complimented me on my boobs.

We hit it off and I still speak to Tanya now and whenever I see the other girls we always catch up. They made it really easy and quite natural for me.

That scene was just a little chat and they invited me to a party that night, which I'm sure they were told to, and that's how I became a part of the show.

The soiree that evening was the Decadence Ball. I entered the bash with Tanya and there I met the rest of the cast.

While filming the show, I got on with the other girls and there were no negatives other than the schedule, which was a bit all over the place. The producers would ask me to film at the last minute, which didn't really work with the children.

But the team were understanding and knew I couldn't just drop my kids off somewhere and start shooting. That's the main reason I remained as a guest Housewife, because I just couldn't commit to full-time. I did consider it – I contemplated upgrading to full-time many times, but logistically it just wasn't possible with the kids.

People find it strange that I don't have help with the children at home. They just assume that I do and say things like, "Can't the nanny look after the kids?" But because of the abuse I suffered as a child I've found it hard to allow anyone to care for my children, which is understandable, I guess. I'm not saying everyone is a paedophile, but my abuser was a trusted person and everyone thought he was lovely and great, so I have that worry there when trying to find someone – do they just seem nice on the surface?

Jo, my housekeeper, is one of the closest people to our family, she's been with us for years. She loves the children and they love her. But I haven't got nannies, where I can go, "Right, I'm going to work. You have the kids." But we would like to have more help in the future.

Patrick and I have talked about it for years, and I haven't found the right person. But then again, I'm not really looking because it scares me.

It is my problem more than anyone else's. My husband would have someone in a heartbeat and would employ five staff if we needed it, to make life easier. I guess it's a motherly instinct and I'm being over-protective, but I'm never going to leave them until I'm completely comfortable. At the moment, I'll go out for a couple of hours here and there and the children will stay with my mum or Patrick. I need to get over that hurdle of letting others in.

If I want to work or continue any kind of career, I need more time available, and therefore more help with childcare.

Luckily, being a guest Housewife meant I wasn't in every single scene, and I dipped in and out of every series I was part of. But what you see on telly is a condensed 45-minute episode, which actually took weeks of filming. On TV, it all seems really dramatic, chaotic and quite full-on. And it was all of that, but we'd filmed it over time and the big scenes were cut down considerably.

It was quite intense at times, but I never got involved in the drama. For me, just being in the room was enough when it was all kicking off. And if there were any big arguments, I'd leave. I wasn't interested in all of that. I just wanted a laugh, to have fun, dress up and go to events.

Everyone asks if the show is scripted. It's not, but things are set up. You're not told what to say, but you might be given topics of conversation to talk about.

"Oh, can somebody discuss what she said to her," the producers would tell us.

And it was those things I didn't really like, because although you weren't told what to say, you were asked to talk about something you wouldn't normally gossip about in real life. But I never relayed that to Patrick. If there were ever any arguments or anything I didn't like, I would never come back and complain about it, because I never wanted him to turn around and go, "Don't do it then."

He'd never watched the show. He didn't know what we were doing, how we were dressed, what we were talking about… and that's the way I decided to keep it.

Then there were the 'parties'. A lot of the time they weren't real parties, and that was a bit disappointing for me, because I just wanted to get out of the house and have a good time. But you'd turn up and there wouldn't even be any music playing on most occasions. There would also be extras standing around, pretending to be having a great time, when actually, no one knew anyone there.

It is a TV show at the end of the day, but the fallouts you watched on-screen were real.

It took me well over a year to try and fit in with the other cast. I filmed four series of Housewives and it was probably the third and fourth when I finally felt I could speak freely.

When making my final series, series 11 of the show, I knew deep down it was probably my last, so I thought, *I'm going to try and enjoy it and get involved.*

We went on a trip to Athens, and I was determined to go for it. All the girls were there for a week, whereas I just joined them for a couple of days. We had a brilliant time. I'm so glad that's where I left it, because I ended it on a high.

Leaving the show in 2020 felt like the right decision, because it just didn't fit in with my life anymore.

The Real Housewives Of Cheshire was so far-removed from my everyday hectic life, and if I'm being honest, I was doing it for a bit of respite.

I always wanted to be very careful and make sure I wasn't quitting the show just because Patrick wanted me to. Although, I'm sure he was over the moon about it when I did eventually leave. At the end of every series he'd ask me not to go back.

But I'd got to the point where I'd got everything I wanted out of it, and I felt there wasn't much more I could give or do. It was also hard keeping up the pretence. I found it really challenging going in and pretending to be at someone's party, who I didn't even know. But the most important reason for leaving was my desire to move on to other things, like my campaigning, which can make a real difference.

It was nevertheless still a hard decision to give up my spot as a guest Housewife, mainly because my biggest fear is being stuck indoors again.

I isolated myself throughout my teenage years and all of my twenties, and I never want to go back to that. I still try and make the most of every single minute I'm out, whether that be when I'm working, or, on the rare occasion, seeing friends.

I'd never mixed with anybody before joining the show. I didn't have any friends, and I never really got glammed up. It was good for me to do something, but I really did suffer with mum guilt. I'd never left the children before, and it was hard to be apart from them, even for just a few hours at a time.

I'm still trying to find the balance now, because I shouldn't feel guilty. I'm entitled to get up and go out, and I was working, which is so important for the children to see.

I'd never say never to returning to the show, and they still ask me to go back and tell me I'm welcome any time.

But I'm busy with other stuff now, and I want to do more. But I'm so grateful for it. Not only did it give me some liberty in my life, it's also where I met my now best friend, Adam. He was a bit like me and a guest on the show. As soon as I met him, we just clicked and laughed so much. My best times and memories from Housewives are when I was filming with Adam. Now, three years later, he's my closest friend.

We had such a good time, and I had my first holiday away from home with him. He's hilarious and we just laugh.

After leaving Housewives, I started going on Loose Women more, which is great because I can talk a lot about autism there, which is why I do everything I do and why I'm so keen to raise my profile. Ultimately, everything I do is for my children.

Now I'm involved in work that Patrick approves of, things are much better. If I say I'm going on Loose Women, he's thrilled. If I'm ever doing anything for charity, he's supportive of that. He'll do his best to be available to care for the children when I'm working, but the real difficulty is balancing our diaries. You can't think about who is financially more important, and I think it's imperative for both parents to work.

But I don't think either of us were quite prepared for the amazing opportunities that came my way after leaving the glitz and glamour of being a Cheshire Housewife behind.

17

Christine McGuinness, Celebrity?

After leaving Housewives, I concentrated on other work. Mainly charity, but I also made appearances on shows like Loose Women and This Morning to talk about the children.

I was no stranger to the odd TV appearance and had made a few small-screen cameos before I'd joined Housewives. Patrick and I did little bits of TV together early on in our relationship as his profile was growing. It was mostly game shows like Who Wants To Be A Millionaire, All Star Mr & Mrs and The Million Pound Drop.

But it was his job and I was just there as his partner.

There was no big boom in my career off the back of it, and I didn't have social media at the time, so it wasn't like

I received a surge in followers. But we always did really well together and won every show we went on. We raised an incredible £275,000 for charity on The Million Pound Drop.

This was all before we had children. Once we did have them, we never really appeared on any more shows together. I never went on TV on my own, not that I wasn't approached. I just wanted to be a mum at home.

Loose Women had asked me a couple of times to go on as a guest, but I always declined because I wasn't sure what I wanted to do. I was just a stay-at-home mum, and I wasn't looking to be working in modelling or TV.

But I had a change of heart when they invited me on to talk about my anorexia. It stemmed from an Instagram post that blew up. I was new to the social media world at the time, and I uploaded a photo of me looking quite ripped and muscular.

Someone said something like, "You need to eat. It's not right to look like that after you've had children."

So, I replied to this uninformed person.

"I'm actually the fittest and healthiest I've ever been. I'm actually training and eating really well," I snapped back.

And it's true, I was at the time.

They then commented back, "You look anorexic to me."

"Do your research. I myself suffered with an eating disorder as a teenager, and at my lowest point I often thought about ending my life," I said.

"I wish someone had taught me about the benefits that healthy eating and exercise can give you on the inside and on the outside of your body a lot sooner.

"I wish I had seen more photos promoting health and fitness, instead of all the 'skinny photos' that did and still do cover our magazines."

I was quite innocent to social media and probably had something like 100 followers. I didn't realise anyone would look at it, or that the press would even know my name.

Someone picked up on the story and before I knew it, it was splashed across a news website. From there, I started getting press and publicity off the back of it, which was never my intention. As a result, Loose Women asked me to go on and talk about my experiences. Amid this media storm, I'd just found out the twins were autistic, but I wasn't ready to discuss that publicly yet.

But I thought, if I do choose to speak about it, Loose Women would be an amazing platform to do so.

Unbeknown to anyone else, I actually used my first time on the show, where I opened up about my anorexia, as a little trial for myself to see how I'd find it, because I'd never done telly on my own before.

The whole time I was thinking to myself, *if this goes OK and I feel comfortable, then a few months later I'll come back and talk about autism.*

And that's what I did. I felt really relaxed on that first occasion. The team were lovely, and the response was really good. The ladies were all so welcoming to me and eventually, when I did reveal the children have autism, they were the first to ring up and say, "Will she come on and talk to us?" I agreed straight away.

We've built up a really good relationship from there. I've appeared on the show over ten times and I've been a guest panellist, too.

One of my proudest moments was when we did the world's first autism-friendly live TV show.

That was absolutely amazing. I was very involved in the organisation of it all, and I advised the producers and presenters on what to do.

It was simple little things, like turning the lights down, having a reduced audience and no music playing. And we discussed autism for the full hour. It was incredible, and nothing had ever been done like that on TV before.

From being a regular on Loose Women, things snowballed, and my public profile gained a bit of a boost. I've since made other appearances and been interviewed on daytime shows like This Morning and Good Morning Britain.

These days, it's not unusual for me to get a phone call asking me to go on TV. It's great, but in true Christine style I'm trying to work out where I fit in.

I'm really comfortable talking about autism and the children, but I'm still undecided about reality TV shows.

It's mainly because programmes like Housewives don't

really fit in with my real life, and because of another experience I'm hesitant to talk about, but I will.

Off the back of my climbing profile – I mean, I say that but I've never really considered myself as well-known – I was approached to go on another TV show. I'm not going to name the show in my book, because it was one of the worst experiences of my life. Not literally, but it was pretty awful.

It was the first programme I was asked to go on as a 'celebrity'. Everything I'd done up until then was about autism, and I was there as a mum talking about my experiences and raising awareness.

But on this particular show, I was there as Christine McGuinness – no husband, or children. I was really unsure, because I don't see myself as a celebrity, I see myself as a mum.

I spoke to my management and said, "I'm really not sure." But then I'm up for a laugh and I love comedy and this show, from what I'd read, had good banter and was a bit of fun. I thought, *I'll just go for it. I'll go and get myself out for the day*. I wanted to push myself out of my comfort zone.

When I arrived at the studios, I felt a bit out of place and I wasn't sure if anyone knew who I was. Then there was the added pressure of being among other celebrity guests, who had a much bigger profile than me.

Anyhow, I put on a brave face and began filming. On this show, you take it in turns to go up for your round, and I was last.

I was a bit anxious, but they'd invited me on after all, so what's the worst that could happen? Nervously, I left my position among the other celebs and walked up to the podium for my turn.

As I waited with baited breath, the co-host came on and in front of everybody exploded into a rant.

"I've got no fucking idea who you are," she said. "I don't care who you are. I don't know who you think you are, and I don't know what you're even doing here."

I was mortified, embarrassed and humiliated. I felt so shit! They were all the things I was questioning myself, and she said everything I was feeling.

I was trying to prepare myself for something like, "Oh, what do you see in your multi-millionaire husband?" And I'd psyched myself up for a bit of a roasting, but not, "Who are you? What are you doing here? Oh, let me have a Google."

I just wanted the ground to swallow me up.

"Oh no. I'm only kidding. I'm actually a massive fan of your husband," she carried on.

This was all in front of the other celebrities. I was very aware that they were all more well-known than me, but everyone starts somewhere. I know it was meant to be a laugh and a bit of fun, but I didn't expect to feel so small. It was horrible.

My natural coping mechanism is to laugh things off, so I giggled along and said, "I really liked you."

But she went on and on.

"Oh, I know who you are," she said.

"Just fucking stop now!" my brain screamed.

"You are really beautiful, aren't you? But there's nothing else."

Stunned, I just replied, "Stop it, that's not nice. I really liked you."

As soon as the cameras stopped rolling, the presenter who went into this massive tirade of insults marched over to me.

"I'm so sorry," she said.

"It's just part of the show, we have to have banter."

I thought, *no, because there are five other celebrities here and you didn't say anything negative to anybody else.*

But to keep the peace, and because I'm not confrontational in the slightest, I replied, "Oh no, it's OK. It's fine."

One of the directors also came to check I was alright afterwards. I guess, as much as I tried to hide my devastation, it was obvious I was absolutely mortified.

I'm glad my grilling was towards the end of the show, as I would have been miserable throughout the episode if I'd been given that dressing down at the start. And by the time we wrapped, I couldn't wait to leave.

I returned to my hotel shaken and in floods of tears – I've never cried so much!

I rang my husband, sobbing. I was just so upset. I know it's stupid, but I can't help but think, *no, that's not right, you shouldn't be like that to a guest on your show. I didn't ask to go on it – I was invited.*

I was really upset about it and ever since then it's always been a focus in my mind. Do I actually want to be on TV? Is this for me?

Do I want to stay as a TV personality? Or just carry on as a campaigner and do something really good, because ultimately that's my goal.

But actually, do I want to be a celebrity? That's something I'm not sure of because that little experience wasn't nice, and it wasn't even all that bad when you think about it.

A while after the show, the presenter in question sent me a long message of apology on Instagram.

"I'm a big fan of your husband, and I think you're amazing," she said.

I didn't reply, and I haven't spoken to her since. I'm not a bully and don't pick on anybody, so I don't want to associate myself with someone like that.

When it came to the series airing, I begged my manager to ask the producers to cut that section out of the edit.

In hindsight, I don't think they would have used it anyway. The presenter would have received a lot of backlash, because it was so harsh and unnecessary. But part of me thought if they did leave that hideous part in, yes, it would have been embarrassing, but it would have exposed her for how nasty she really was.

And she'll know my name, don't worry. They'll invite

me back on and I'll say no. Sadly, not everyone in this world can be pleasant.

Trolling can be quite rampant for those in the public eye, but I'm so lucky that I've never experienced it badly, since that person called me anorexic. My followers are all amazing and really support female empowerment.

Some of the stuff I put online can be quite racy at times, but for me, I'm just doing a job. I'm telling you, I'm really not that sexy!

But I'm lucky I've got a nice supportive group of followers that will go, "Yes, go on girl."

I do feel quite lucky considering I've done a handful of TV shows and have been on social media for a few years, yet I've only had that one horrific experience. And the good always outweighs the bad.

One of my most incredible moments was when I landed a job to model for Ann Summers. As a teenager, once I put the pageant side of things behind me and moved on to lingerie stuff, I knew I never wanted to do glamour and get my boobs out, but I became quite comfortable doing sexy stuff.

The Ann Summers gig could have totally backfired, and I wouldn't have been surprised if someone said, "Put it away, you're a mum and you're doing underwear modelling." But for me, I'm just doing a job and other celebrities like Naomi Campbell and Jennifer Lopez are in their fifties and are mums and modelling, so why shouldn't I?

Still, I always have that little knot in my tummy before I upload something on social media and think, *oh God, I'm going to get trolled*.

The Ann Summers job really was a dream come true, and it's a high-street brand I've always been really loyal to. I remember their shop windows being flawlessly stunning.

The models were beautiful, the whole creative side of it was on point and the photoshoots were always amazing.

I'm obsessed with gorgeous lingerie anyway, because of the way it makes you feel. If I've got a matching set on and it's stunning and fits right, I instantly feel better.

I've always been an Ann Summers fan, but I never thought I'd model for them – especially after having kids. I'd just succumbed to the prospect that my days in front of the camera were well and truly over.

So, you can imagine how unreal it felt to become the first mum ever to do a campaign with them, which is just mad. What's even crazier is that I didn't even say yes straight away.

My initial reaction was, "What? No! I can't do that." Of course, I wanted to, but it's the self-doubt in me. Straight away I was thinking, *I'm 33, I've got twins, I've got a C-section scar and look a bit tired – can I still model?* It's a bit of a double life.

After mulling it over, I agreed to do it. I thought, *I can't say no, this is a photoshoot I've dreamt of doing all my life. Even if I don't look the way I did when I had these dreams, it's still my dream. They must be OK with me doing it, or they wouldn't have asked me.*

But right up until the day of shooting, I was ringing my management saying, "I don't think I can do it. I'm just not in great shape." It was after two lockdowns and I hadn't been to the gym for a year and my hair was awful, because I couldn't go to a hairdresser. I'd been colouring it myself at home. It's safe to say I was feeling less than glamorous.

But I sucked it up and went for it, and on that two-day shoot I was so well looked after. I also got the chance to meet Ann Summers' CEO, Jacqueline Gold. She's a massive inspiration to me because she's had breast cancer, got through that, is a business powerhouse and a really strong, empowering woman. She walked in the room where we were shooting and instantly had this aura where she was almost untouchable.

Jacqueline gets my love for gorgeous lingerie and how it makes women feel. I think that's why she's so successful. She's passionate about making women feel good, and that's why she creates this stunning underwear. I couldn't believe she asked me to model it for her.

The photoshoot was great fun. We even filmed a choreographed dance routine for the campaign, with a couple of the other stunning girls who were modelling, too.

Patrick approved of the pictures as well. When it came to psyching myself up for the photoshoot, he asked me, "Are you sure you want to do it?"

Being photographed in sexy underwear was never a problem for him, because right from when I first met him, I'd always done lingerie modelling, so he's used to it. In fact, the first time he met me I was in a bikini!

More than anything, he knew I wasn't feeling very confident at the time and suggested that I deferred it to the next year when I was more comfortable.

"No, what if they don't ask me again?" I said to him. It's one of those rare things that's a once-in-a-lifetime opportunity, so I couldn't risk losing out for good.

I'm so glad I went for it, because I love the pictures and it'll be so amazing when I'm older to be able to say I modelled for Ann Summers. It goes to show you should never give up on your dreams, and it's one of the biggest jobs of my career.

In terms of TV, the jury's still out. I get asked all the time if I'd do other reality shows, and I'm constantly rumoured to be going in the jungle or on Strictly Come Dancing.

Truth be told, I'd love to do the majority of those shows. But, as with everything in my life, my children come first. I can't commit to something really full-on just yet. I simply can't jump on a plane and go to Australia for a month. I'd need a lot of notice to prep the children. Ten years ago, before I had the kids, I actually met with the jungle producers. I can't remember what happened, but for whatever reason I didn't do it.

I know that back then I'd have just been the bikini girl in

the shower, and I probably wouldn't have gained any good jobs afterwards. But now I'm older and wiser, and I have so much more to talk about.

If I'd gone in the jungle all those years ago, I probably wouldn't have lasted long in the industry either, because I was super-sensitive in those days. I'm still really soft, and I haven't got a thick skin. But I help myself by not reading comments on news sites, and I don't Google myself. Overnight success unfortunately isn't all it's cracked up to be. It might seem fun at the time, but from what I've seen as an outsider, it can be quite damaging.

However there is one thing I'm working on which is a bit of a dive in the deep-end for shy and unconfident me. While writing my book, I've started filming for The Real Full Monty on ITV, which is amazing because it's all in aid of breast cancer awareness, a cause so close to my heart.

Don't get me wrong, I'm nervous and have never done anything like this before, but it's great to be able to make a difference. And I'll be able to meet some new people. It'll also be a bit of a break from everyday life. I often find going to work is easier than staying at home with the children sometimes. A day on set is like a day off for me, and I want to continue working. Even though my husband is doing so well with his career and financially, I've still got that part of me where I want to earn and have my own independence.

I'm still turning down big jobs because I've not got childcare. But I still can't believe I'm being offered this work – or the amount of money. It's just not where I've come from. Saying no to work when you know what it's like to have nothing is really hard. But I decline these opportunities to be with my children, and that's something money can't buy.

It's a double-edged sword, because my husband is doing well, but everything could be cancelled tomorrow. We've both got it in us where we want to work and earn money. Especially with our children, we don't know what their future is going to be and if we're going to have to provide extra money or support. But I'm living my thirties as best as I can, and saying yes to as many opportunities as possible. I really do believe you can have it all – be a mum, wife, have a career and a social life. You might be exhausted, but you can do it. And thankfully, I have a really good and understanding management who support me and book me in some really lovely work.

Before meeting my now manager Claire Powell at the CAN Group, I had a model agent. And in my early twenties I signed to a local Liverpool publicist, Leisa Maloney.

Leisa and I became quite close, and I worked with her for around ten years. She was brilliant and so understanding, but I could never take on much work. She'd always offer it to me, but it was always me saying no. I didn't feel that confident, and my husband didn't really want a wife in the public eye, which he made quite clear. I suppose I chose to be a wife instead of having a career.

Leisa was always at the end of the phone if I needed her, but I was busy being a mum and, in those days, I wanted to stay in with the children – you know how over-the-top obsessed I was with them. But she was there for me 100 per cent when I needed her. She's still a friend, and I'm really glad she's in my life.

I met Claire in 2019, when I went to an event for Caudwell Children – a charity that supports autistic children as well as other illnesses in children

I was always sent invites to Caudwell events but was never able to go, because of the children. However, on this occasion they were opening a huge Autism centre abd it was during the daytime, while the kids were at school. It was also only an hour away from home. So, to my delight, I was able to attend the opening of this autism centre. There were lots of celeb guests there, including Peter Andre who was there with his wife Emily. For me, that was mad because he was my first-ever crush when I was in junior school. I remember his biggest hit, Mysterious Girl, had just come out. It was the first time I looked at a man and realised what fancying someone was. I watched the music video and went, "Oh, he's lovely."

But he's an absolute gentleman and we always catch up when we see each other at events. He was there with Claire, who is also his manager, and she asked me to come over for a little chat. We were talking about the kids more than anything, and I did not think in a million years she was thinking about becoming my manager. We just got on really well and chatted about autism. Later, as I was leaving, she asked who was managing me and what I was doing for work.

"I'm not working, I'm a mum," I told her.

"But you could do so much! You've got so much potential," she told me, reassuringly.

I never believed her and I've been so astounded by the things that have come my way, since I signed with Claire after that event. I never thought I would have my own book, film a BBC documentary and head up a campaign with Ann Summers. All these things seemed worlds apart from my life at home with the children.

From the beginning, I made it clear to my agency I wanted to do charity work. I've been with CAN management for two years now, and I'm an ambassador for the charity that connected us.

I must say, I was shocked when the founder of the charity John Caudwell asked me to be an ambassador. I was so happy because I knew how much of a juggernaut the charity was and I felt so passionate in helping autistic children and I could see John was too.

Supporting great causes has always been so important to me, and that's what I've continued to do. Particularly raising awareness for autism and breast cancer. My work for the latter has increased over the last year. It became a cause even closer to my heart when my own mother was diagnosed with an aggressive form of the disease.

18

Making A Difference

It was my brother, Jamie, who sat me down and told me Mum has cancer.

I knew there was a risk – she'd been complaining about a lump on her breast for four months. Mum had done the sensible thing and visited a doctor, but she'd been told she was fine and sent away.

But her lump gradually got bigger. And as the bulge grew, so did our concern, because four of my aunties previously had breast cancer, one of whom sadly passed away from the awful disease.

So, she went back to see a different nurse, a few months later in 2020, who straight away said, "With your family history alone, you should have been sent for a full examination."

The next day she was booked in for a scan and then a lumpectomy was arranged.

When she went to hospital for a mammogram, the specialist oncologist checked her over and told her some devastating news.

"I'd be really shocked if this isn't cancer," he said. "We have to wait for your biopsy results to confirm, but to me I think I'm looking at cancer."

When she relayed this to me over the phone, I still had hope that it might not be the big C, because he still needed the biopsy back to confirm for definite.

Obviously, he knew what he was looking at, but I was desperately hoping that maybe it wasn't what I was dreading. I kept thinking to myself, *she's too healthy, she doesn't look poorly and she's not ill*. She seemed great, other than being a bit tired and having a lump. Maybe I was in denial.

While she was waiting for the confirmed results, I drove to her house to pick her up. Jamie still lives with my mum in Halewood, and she was upstairs when we started chatting.

"You do know that this is cancer," he told me.

"It might not be," I replied.

And he said, "No, it is. They've given her a Macmillan nurse."

I didn't want to believe it, but not long after that the results came back and she was diagnosed as HER2-positive, which is a rare form of breast cancer and it was aggressive, to say the least.

But the team got straight on it and she was booked in to have her lump removed, and then a course of extensive chemotherapy.

Like a trooper, she underwent her treatment with a smile on her face.

But behind the scenes I was devastated that I couldn't be there for her.

It was in the middle of the pandemic, and not only was I not allowed onto the oncology wards, but her immune system was so weak that the risk of Covid was too great, so I couldn't see her at all.

For her to go through winter and chemo without her family around her was awful. It was hard to accept her diagnosis, but then there was the added heartbreak of not being able to be there for her.

Nevertheless, Mum's very much like me. She's a strong woman and really positive, and she was protected in a way, because no one was allowed near her.

But it was just dreadful. It's something I'll never get my head around, that I couldn't be there for Mum when she was going through chemotherapy. All I could do was speak to her every single day on the phone, and try to make her laugh. But it was a bitter pill to swallow.

She's been there for me throughout my whole life. She's been the biggest help with my children. She's been by my side throughout my marriage difficulties and my career. And she's been my greatest cheerleader. But when she was going through chemotherapy, I couldn't be there to hold her hand and give her a cuddle. I really missed her, and the children did too.

Mum only saw them once in nine months, and it was a huge loss for us all, because she's normally such a massive part of the kids' routines.

On our visual calendar we have at home, it had her face next to every single weekend. In turn, the kids always knew Nanny was coming on Saturdays, and we'd do something together as a family. Since having the children, Mum and I would do all the outings together, right from when they were toddlers.

My husband would be working, or he'd struggle to deal with them when out and about. And there was the added challenge of him potentially getting recognised, which would make things even more difficult. So, any playgroups we went to, swimming sessions or trips to the park, it was always Mum and I who took the kids. It was extremely hard for all of us to have those things stopped overnight. The heartbreaking thing is the children have got used to it now.

They used to ask every weekend, "When's Nanny coming?" And it's quite sad that they don't bring it up anymore.

We're hoping to get back to some kind of routine soon. I don't think Mum can come over every weekend so quickly after treatment, but when she starts feeling better, I'd like her to come round – but only when she's ready. She's worried about the children seeing her with such short hair, following the chemo.

The one time she did visit she wore a wig and the kids didn't notice, but she was really worried about scaring the children. It's been so tough, but it's one of those hurdles in life that makes you strong and appreciate everything more.

All through her battle with cancer, Mum was so brave. They've removed the lump now, and she's had the most chemo you can possibly have. But she powered through and finished her treatment at the end of March, and in April she completed a course of radiotherapy. That was given to her as an added precaution to reduce the chances of the cancer returning.

Although, the medical staff keep warning her the aggressive cancer she has could come back, and it wants to. She's not out of the woods just yet. She still has hormone injections once a month, and that will be ongoing for a couple of years, but she's in remission, looking stronger and has more energy. Her hair is slowly growing back, too.

It was a really difficult time for all of us as a family and throughout it all, the thing that was prominent on my mind was the children. They haven't got any other grandparents and they need their nanny.

To take some positives from our experience, my mum's story had a massive impact on other people. She asked me to share her tale on social media, and I'm so glad she did because the response has been overwhelming.

The number of messages I got on that first day of telling my followers was incredible. I had so many DMs from people saying things like, "Thank you for talking about it and letting people know this can happen to anyone."

I got a lot of words of support from other daughters about how they felt about their mums going through it, because when you're in the midst of it you don't really know who to talk to or how to feel.

When someone you love gets cancer, you sympathise and feel awful for them, but you have this feeling inside you that is permanently petrified of losing them. But you're scared to say it or feel it, because you have to be strong for the other person.

I never rang my mum up in tears saying, "I don't want to lose you." I never would have done that. My job was to phone her, make her laugh, tell her everything's fine and that we're all OK without her while she concentrates on her treatment. You've got to be the strong one sometimes, as hard as it may be.

It was good talking about it with my lovely followers, and it was comforting to hear from other people who said they weren't sure how to deal with it either. You feel awful for feeling upset about it, when it's not you going through it, but you sort of are. Inside, you're absolutely heartbroken. The thought of losing her when they said it's aggressive, and the fact it could travel or come back somewhere else, is hard to bear.

But these are all just possibilities. You could live every day feeling down or upset, but you're only wasting your own time.

You've got to carry on, stay positive and keep fighting. And thank God she has. She's done so well, and hopefully she's going to be around much longer. I can't imagine not having my mum by my side. I keep saying to her, "It's not your time yet, we're not finished with you, you can't go."

She really can't go, because the kids need her. It's funny, she always says she's a much better nan than she was a mum. And I think most people are. It's a second chance to learn from your own mistakes.

And being a bit older and wiser, she's put lots of effort into making sure she's a good nan to the children, and she's been brilliant. Since I've had the kids, she's been the best mum, too. She's always there for us all.

There's no one in the world I trust with my kids more than my mum, and that's something you can't buy.

She might give them too much chocolate and mess up their routine, like a lot of grandparents do. But I know my children are safe with Mum, and they won't come to any harm. I have missed having her around for that stability I haven't got with anyone else.

She's 'Nutty Nanny' and she doesn't take life too seriously. She's always been a bit of a free spirit.

Leo, Penelope and Felicity definitely have a special bond with Mum, they just love her to bits.

It's hard to even entertain that she might not have made it through, because I don't know how I would have coped without her these last few years. She's been such a rock for us when we've been through difficult times, like when the kids were diagnosed with autism. She made things feel a bit lighter, so when she had cancer, I had to do that for her.

But during the difficult time of Mum's battle with cancer, I had some decisions to make. I knew there was a strong risk that I could develop breast cancer myself at some point, because of my family history.

I'd thought about having a BRCA test, which tests for the breast cancer gene, for a while anyway and my mum getting cancer confirmed that I had to do it, now more than ever. I need to be around for my children for as long as possible and if that meant I was required to have a double mastectomy to reduce my chances of developing cancer, I was fully prepared to do it.

Actually doing the test was another story. I put off having it for so long because I was terrified what the results might be. But it was something my husband encouraged me to do, too. He has a history of heart problems in his family and goes for regular check-ups himself.

So, reluctantly, I went and got tested. It was all very easy, a simple swab test, and the results were sent to my GP. I didn't tell my mum about it until after I got the results, as I didn't want to put that extra worry on her.

Many weeks of anguish and worry later, I got the results. It was negative. I felt so relieved. I mean, nothing's for certain and the doctor explained to me it doesn't mean I'll never get cancer, but it just provides that added reassurance that my chances are just the same as everyone else's. Everyone was so delighted for me, Mum especially, and that was a little reason for us to celebrate amid the storm of tough times.

It's been a mix of highs and lows the last year, but to add another sprinkle of beauty to this nightmare, I was recently offered the chance to become an ambassador for The Pink Ribbon Foundation. I accepted the opportunity straight away, because I've always supported them and they really do amazing work.

When I started working with them, I spoke to the head of the charity, Lisa, on the phone.

"Regardless of what's happened with your mum, you've supported us for years," she told me.

"It makes sense for you to be an ambassador."

And it's true, because of the history of breast cancer in our family, I've always raised money for The Pink Ribbon Foundation.

As a teenager, I regularly cleared out my bedroom and put on car boot sales. I also sold clothes and hosted fashion shows, coffee mornings and ladies' lunches.

And now, I always put charity work above my own paid work. I never accept a fee from a charity, the money will always go to the trust. Even the documentary we've been filming for the BBC, we've donated our whole fee to the National Autistic Society.

Supporting charity is so crucial to everything I do, and I guess that comes from my own childhood. From a young age, Mum drummed into us that helping charities is something we must do.

Because as a low-income family, we relied on the kind-hearted generosity of others ourselves. Furniture was always given to us by the council or was second hand. Our clothes were mostly second hand or hand-me-downs, too. So, I'll always do everything in my power to support charity as much as I can.

You've got to raise awareness, and I'd like to think somewhere along the way, I've helped people. Well, I know I have.

I've had messages from parents who've said their children have been diagnosed with autism because of things I've said, which is my ultimate goal – helping others and making a better world for my children.

It's weird really, because throughout my life I've always been a bit of a floater. You can probably tell now you've reached this far into my book. I've always just gone along with things, so I haven't quite found where I'm supposed to be yet, but there's still time. And in my life now more than ever I feel more determined to keep working, but I'm not sure what direction I'm going in. Most importantly, with everything I'm doing this year – writing the book and filming the documentary, for example – there's some good behind it.

And charity is always at the forefront of all the work I do. I'm so grateful and glad the jobs I'm doing now are all focused around raising awareness, money and understanding. It's a really fulfilling thing to be doing and there's also a lot of fun to be had with it as well.

I guess if my 18-year-old self could see me now, well, I would say it's beyond my wildest dreams, but I always had goals and ambitions. I always knew I was going to get out of Halewood. It wasn't that I wanted to be famous, or for anyone to know my name. I just knew I wanted to be successful, a mum and a strong woman.

The best thing I'm doing now is inspiring, encouraging and educating others. I can't believe the girl who left school at 14 with no GCSEs – who was constantly told they'd never amount to anything and would end up pregnant in a council flat – is now on TV talking about autism.

And I'm so proud to say I've raised over a million pounds for charity, and that's my greatest accomplishment. There have been so many projects for important causes I've worked on over my limited time in the public eye.

I took part in a sports challenge, which was a week of fitness activities like cycling and bodyweight exercises, for the National Autistic Society and that raised a quarter of a million pounds alone. I'm just so proud I did that.

I opened the very first autism centre in Belfast. I still can't believe my name is on a plaque outside – that's amazing.

I've been nominated for my first ever award – a National Diversity Award. And that's all to do with my work for charity and raising awareness for autism.

These are all things I never could have imagined I would achieve, but it's the best thing – better than any TV show I've been part of or any other work that I've done. The money I've raised is more important to me than anything. It gives you a purpose. I know I've been fortunate with my husband's career and what he's given to our family and the life he's provided, but to change other people's lives is one step greater. I also feel like it's helped keep our feet firmly on the ground.

When you come from nothing, and then you're doing well, you could easily get swept up in it. You could fall into the trap of thinking you're someone special, and having autistic children has really kept us really grounded. It's been such a huge blessing and I'm so grateful for the kiddies. It's been difficult and challenging, but my whole life has been a bit like that.

Supporting causes that are so in need of awareness and funding is so important to do and I love doing it and knowing that we can help. It's one of those things we never speak about. I don't go around telling people, "I've raised a million pounds for charity."

Actually, I don't think I've ever said it out loud until

now, but I think it's great to help others. I'm lucky that I work very closely with a lot of charities as well as The Pink Ribbon Foundation.

The first time I was asked to be an ambassador was for the National Autistic Society, and that happened when we first revealed the children have autism.

They got in touch and asked if we needed any support or advice, so we met up with them. After working with the guys there and getting involved in various charity events, they asked me to become an ambassador, which means you represent the charity and raise awareness. You're there to support and help.

An ambassador role is their way of saying thank you for helping and you're important to us. It's nice to be appreciated and it's such an honour. I've been working with them for four years now.

Then last year I was made an ambassador for Caudwell Children, which is a perfect fit for me. At first, I was unsure whether to accept, because I get asked to be an ambassador for so many charities and I can't possibly do them all.

I told my manager, Claire, that I was worried about taking on the role for two charities which are quite similar and both support autistic children. As desperately as I want to support them as much as I can, I need to be able to give my time to each.

If I'm an ambassador, I don't want to have to say no when they ask me to help.

But I've been going to Caudwell events for years and I know how much they put into looking after children just like mine, so I really believe in what they do. And I agreed to join their team.

There have been so many pinch-me moments along the way, but one of my most memorable and proudest moments was when I organised my very own ball, named Twinkle Ball, to raise money for the National Autistic Society. Although it turned out to be an incredible night and raised lots of funds for charity, it didn't come without its fair share of drama.

I guess the first error was organising it all without telling Patrick. I didn't inform him of the ball until the last minute because we had so much going on at the time.

It was just before I joined Housewives, and when our marriage was all over the papers. I had it in my head that I wanted to do something to help autism. At this point, everyone knew our children were autistic, so I thought, *right, I want to throw a ball to give back.*

It was before we knew Felicity was autistic, but we'd had the twins' diagnoses, so we named it after them – our Twinkles.

I just went off and arranged it all on my own accord.

I booked the venue, the acts, got the sound system sorted and sold hundreds of tickets through a public relations company. I even had the invitations written up professionally. But the hardest part was when it came to telling my husband.

Making A Difference

I just WhatsApped him the invite with the message, "Do you mind hosting this event for me?" I'd never done anything like it before in my life.

That was in early February. I'd already done all the advertising and sold the tickets, and the ball was due to take place in the April. Then, of course, that dreadful March happened.

For those few weeks, no one knew what was happening. Were we going together or was I attending on my own?!

It was awful, because I'd arranged this amazing glitzy ball, and spent so much time getting everything sorted. It was all for a good cause, and I had no idea what was going on.

Either way, there was no way I was going to let everyone down.

Thank God we were fine by the time we got to April, and we went and hosted our first Twinkle Ball together.

We raised £150,000 that night at the gorgeous Hilton Hotel and it was such a success we did it again a year later. And we surpassed our expectations when it came to the fundraising. On the second evening we totted up £250,000, which was all important cash for the National Autistic Society.

We asked for a helping hand from our celebrity friends such as John Bishop, Jason Manford and Leigh Francis. They all came along to support us, and they offered their comedic skills, too.

Looking back at those two incredible evenings, it was absolutely amazing. I'm not being biased, but of all the charity events I've ever been to, which is a lot, I think ours was the most fun. JLS star Marvin Humes took to the decks for a DJ set on the first event and Rick Astley sang an array of songs on the second.

As well as having loads of fun, of course we told everyone the reason we were there and spoke about the children. I did a little speech on stage, too. My speech wasn't too long, because public speaking is NOT my forte, but I just thanked everyone for coming. The main thing we wanted was for everyone to have a really brilliant time, party, celebrate autism and raise loads of money as well.

We also had a table there that we gave away to parents of autistic children. They were all saying they hadn't had a night out in years and it was the best night they'd ever had.

That was really lovely to hear, because I know how difficult it can be to find the time to get dressed up and go out. It was great to be there with Patrick and do something together and support a cause that champions our children. He also said a few kind words about me on that first evening.

"She's beautiful on the outside but she's even more beautiful on the inside, trust me," he told the crowd.

"What she does for our kids is amazing."

That was really touching.

We haven't been able to organise another ball since, because of the pandemic, but we will again.

Making A Difference

And for Patrick and I, putting on those events did us wonders. As well as raising lots of money for charity and throwing two great balls, it pulled us back together.

19

Confidence

I don't really have many friends in the industry.

I've told you about Adam and another close friend of mine I have to mention is Nelly.

She's a blogger who I first met at an event and we instantly just hit it off. We quickly realised our birthdays are just one day apart, and the fact we're both Pisces is probably why we get on so well.

I have a few others who are close to me that I trust, but when you're in the showbiz world it is hard to make friends, because people are understandably quite guarded. I'm the same myself and I struggle to make friends in this line of work. Having a life in the public eye can be polarising and make you feel paranoid, but I find it hard to be anyone other than me.

I've got quite a dry sense of humour and not everyone gets it, so I'm very aware I could say something and it could be taken the wrong way. That does make you more introverted.

I suppose it can be quite isolating, which isn't great for me, but there's loads of positives that come with it too. You get to go to these amazing events and dress up. Things you wouldn't normally go to in average life.

For example, the Pride Of Britain awards I've been to numerous times and that's a really emotional evening, but there's so much passion and an abundance of inspirational stories. You always come away feeling in awe and inspired from sitting in a room amongst real heroes.

That's the event where I had the biggest pinch-me moment and I can't believe I've been invited to it.

It's not about walking the red carpet or looking glamorous, you're in a room with inspirational and amazing people who have achieved incredible things.

And that night means so much more to me than going to the National Television Awards or BRIT Awards. Yes, those events are full of pop stars and actors and presenters, but it's nothing compared to being amongst people who've saved lives.

One person in this business who I've kept in contact with over the years is The Apprentice and Celebrity Big Brother star Jess Cunningham. She's one of my WhatsApp friends and we voice note each other almost every day. She's always been a great supporter of me and advocates strongly for women in business. She's got five children too and I don't know how she does it – she's like superwoman!

We first met when I was invited to her event called Mother Of Maniacs – The Business And Babies Mindset Event in 2018. She'd organised the bash and it was all about female empowerment. Of course, it was a no-brainer for me to attend, because I love that ethos and it sounded right up my street.

So, I put on a cute little black number, hopped in a cab and went along to support it. Once I arrived at the fancy Menagerie restaurant in Manchester in all my glad rags, I was immediately whisked off upstairs to meet Jess. She was all flappy and said, "Thank you so much for coming. My public speaker's let me down, please will you go on stage and do a speech."

"No! Never in a million years. No way," I said without hesitation. Public speaking is not my thing!

This was before I had a profile in my own right and I hadn't been on Housewives or anything at this point.

And she said, "Please, please, I'll pay you whatever you want!" I was adamant I couldn't do it.

I just wanted to get out of the house for an hour and support women in business, this was the last thing I needed. I've since found out Made In Chelsea's Binky Felstead was the celebrity speaker who had to cancel at the last minute, no doubt for good reasons.

"Please, I'm begging you," she persisted.

"I'm on my arse, I've got no one to speak and I've got 300 people here who have all got tickets to watch someone speak."

And as much as all my instincts were telling me, "No, don't do it," I reluctantly agreed. On stage I was shaking, but I spoke about the children having autism publicly for the first time and the room was silent – you could hear a pin drop. Everyone was listening intently to what I was saying.

At the end of my nervous speech, we held a question and answer session and everyone in the room had their hands up to ask me about it. It was amazing and I'm still so proud I pulled it off.

Unsurprisingly, Jess has invited me to every single event since and I've always said no, unless I can come as a guest. She always laughs that I saved her bacon that night. But it was a success and from that we've become very good friends and she's given me a lot of confidence.

She's always at the end of the phone if I need her. It's amazing how things happen and now if I'm ever struggling with anything work-wise, I'll send Jess a message and she usually puts everything into perspective for me.

Anything personal or where I'm a bit all over the place I'll ring Nelly, but for business stuff I'll ring Jess. She'll usually tell me to go for it, whatever it may be.

That was ideal for me all those years ago, before I joined Housewives, because I only really had my mum and my husband – and both of them were dead against that kind of stuff. Jess has always been so encouraging.

In recent years, I've definitely built my confidence up when it comes to celebrity bashes. And I'll never forget one of the first parties I went to on my own.

It was for celeb psychic Sally Morgan's podcast launch in Camden, London. I was on the guestlist to go because I'd appeared on her show myself talking about autism.

I'd never stayed on my own in London overnight before and I didn't really know anyone in the industry at that time, so I was anxious about the event. I was deliberating whether to attend, but there was this little voice in my head which said, "You're never going to get to know people unless you go." So, I forced myself out of the door.

There were a couple of celebs there that I recognised and I was well acquainted with a few of the guests. Lisa, who I mentioned is head of The Pink Ribbon Foundation, was there and I chatted away to her, and she introduced me to a lady she was with called Laura. Laura's an Instagram blogger known as @thatmumwithcancer, and she keeps her followers updated with her cancer journey. She's been through a lot and has been battling cancer since 2017. I was heartbroken when I found out she's at stage 4.

Laura and her husband were just incredible to talk to and put my anxious mind at ease. We laughed all night and decided to go back to my hotel to the rooftop bar, which is something I'd never done before. Normally, I'd be so shy I wouldn't speak to anyone or I'd leave early, but I was having such a ball that I carried on the party at my hotel. We ordered some food and carried on chatting and giggling. I have such fond memories of that evening and I'm so glad I went against my instincts and showed up.

I've stayed in contact with Laura, too. It was exactly one year later when my mum got diagnosed with cancer and she rang me straight away.

It's amazing how life connects you with people, and if I hadn't been a guest on Sally's podcast, I wouldn't have been there that night and wouldn't have met Laura.

I'm grateful to myself that I went out that evening, because it gave me a lot of confidence to do it again and from there I've gone to other events on my own.

It was certainly a change from years of attending red carpets with my husband as 'Paddy's wife'. Literally no one would speak to me or say hello. I understand it's not a personal thing, no one knew me, whereas *everyone* knew my husband. Those events were quite isolating because I just didn't know anybody. But the only way to get over that was just to go out on my own and mix with people.

It's a crazy world, this entertainment business I'm in. I find it particularly hard, because my insecurities do play havoc with my confidence anyway.

My body is something I'll never be fully confident with. But that's OK, I'm comfortable. These days, I just accept that this is who I am and what I look like.

Confidence

While there's a million things I'd change about myself, I'm sort of OK with accepting this is how I am and I try not to overthink it. There are more important things in life and that's something you realise when you get older and when you've had children. After everything I've been through, I just feel really lucky to be healthy and still here.

Even when I look back at pictures of myself in my twenties, I can't believe how much I stressed and thought I was ugly and out of shape. I spent all those years obsessing over my appearance, so I'm thinking I need to enjoy this time now because in another ten years I'll be looking at myself in my thirties thinking, *I wish I looked like that.*

You can't go on changing yourself forever, and you can't waste time worrying about the outside. It's all about how you feel.

But believe me when I say I'm not confident. I question absolutely everything. I always think I'm not good enough, not just in the way I look, but with everything. With my husband, with work, with this book, absolutely everything. But I'm also at a place where I've got to go for it, because worrying about things isn't going to help me – it's wasting energy on something negative.

So, I'm all for staying positive, moving forward and accepting myself as I am. As long as I'm healthy.

In the past, I've been fixated on my appearance, and after having the twins I did have a boob job. But if I'm honest, I probably only had an enhancement from a 32D to a 32E because I was approached by a cosmetic surgery company.

As an older and wiser woman, I do believe it's wrong that places like that approach girls.

I think it's different if someone wants it, goes to them and they decide to do a deal. But they came to me, and I wasn't thinking about getting my boobs done at all. However, I'd just had the kids, my confidence was on the floor and I got offered free surgery in exchange for a photoshoot, so I accepted.

While I'm happy with my cleavage now, I do often wonder if I would have had them done if I hadn't been contacted by that company.

I'm lucky because my boobs have always been big, but as my weight has gone up and down, my bust has followed suit.

It's sad looking back, because when I was pregnant with the twins, I barely took any photographs of myself. It's one of my biggest regrets. I struggled with the size of my body and I put on six stone during pregnancy.

Now, I'm in a different frame of mind. I'm so proud of my weight gain, and I managed to carry them until full-term. I also had really healthy babies, and both were good weights. I'm so proud of my body for achieving that. And I needn't have panicked, because the weight dropped off afterwards.

Most importantly, I realised the female body is

incredible. And when I got pregnant again with Felicity, I really embraced it and took photos almost every day.

I joined social media in between having the children and I was really happy with my blossoming body.

I liked people following my pregnancy journey, whereas I never did that with the twins. The second time round I thought, *no, it's incredible what women can achieve.* You shouldn't worry about your size and the changes in your physique because you're creating a little person, a little miracle, that's more special than anything.

When it comes to my confidence issues, Patrick is really supportive. But we've been together for 14 years and we don't walk around showering each other with compliments saying, "You look amazing today."

I think I drive him mad because I struggle making decisions and it will be anything from what I should eat to what I should wear. It doesn't matter if I'm going on the school run, out for lunch or attending a red-carpet event, I always want my husband's approval on my outfit and I think it drives him mad. But sometimes he quite enjoys a little fashion show. I can't just choose an outfit and go out, I need him to assure me that it looks good.

That's the lack of confidence in myself. I'm constantly thinking, am I going to choose something nice? So, I'll ask him. He helps me make decisions, which is something I've always struggled with. Even when I used to go shopping with my mum as a teenager, we'd traipse around ten shops trying to find an outfit and I'd always end up back in the first store. And if I like something I'll buy it in every colour, because I hate choosing things.

But slowly, I'm gaining confidence in all areas.

For example, eating out.

When I used to go out to restaurants, I never wanted to be difficult or seen to be complaining, but I'm so particular and I like really dry and plain food. I'd always feel awful asking somebody in an eatery to make sure my fish is well done and without any sauce on it.

So, back in the day the food would arrive prepared as it should be for anybody else, then I wouldn't eat it, or would shove it around the plate. Now when I'm out I'll ask politely, "Do you mind making sure it's cooked well done?" I'll have it as I want it and then I'll enjoy the meal instead of completely skipping it, which is a step forward.

That's something I'll teach the children. Don't worry about being yourself. It's not always complaining if you're asking for something to be done a little bit differently to help you.

When it comes to my eating troubles, I still have my moments and as I previously mentioned, I think I always will.

But I try to follow as healthy a diet as I can, and I became a pescatarian two years ago. That came about while on a weekend trip to Albania with Adam.

He still messages me about that holiday all the time,

because we had such a ball. It was so quiet, the hotel was amazing and we didn't really need to venture outside the grounds of the resort because it was that nice.

We met the owners of the hotel and one evening at dinner, they asked us if we wanted to taste some of the fish that they'd freshly caught. I never ate much fish before then, but the owner of the hotel was insistent and kept saying, "Try this, it's really nice." It was a platter of octopus and all types of seafood I'd never heard of.

He was really pushing me to taste some and part of me was thinking, *is this a cultural thing? I don't want to upset him.* So, I had the tiniest little bite of everything there.

After that, because I ate some of the fish and I liked it, on a whim I decided to become a pescatarian. And I haven't eaten meat since the trip. I previously only had chicken anyway, and I've never tried red meat before. Fish is beige and dry, which is the dream for me – and it's healthy!

Everyone is different with their eating habits, and it's something I speak to Nelly about a lot. Her struggles are the complete opposite to mine, as she has an eating disorder where when she's stressed, she overeats, whereas if I'm stressed, I can't eat at all. We're both so similar but we project our anxieties in different ways.

The thing I've learnt is you don't get sympathy when you struggle to put weight on. While Nelly is so supportive and she gets it, other people say things like, "I wish I looked like you."

If I went online saying, "I've managed to gain a stone in a year, but it's been really difficult," in general, the comments I would get back would be quite sarcastic like, "Oh, poor you."

I don't really speak about it too much for that reason, because you don't get any sympathy.

Not that I need it, but a lot of people don't understand and can be quite judgemental.

It's an ongoing process and I really am trying to gain weight and muscle. But I guess some news I've recently found out explains why I've battled with food aversions all my life.

20

Chameleon

When I first put pen to paper to write this book, I joked that I would have a diagnosis by the time it went to press.

I must have had a premonition or deep down I knew something was coming, because when making the finishing touches to my memoir, I did actually receive a diagnosis.

You may be shocked or you might not be, but I have been confirmed as autistic.

It's strange, but when I read back parts of my book, I noticed there are little hints throughout my life that I'm autistic and more like my children than I ever could have imagined.

My issues with food, my social struggles, how hard I find it to make friends and stay focused, and my indecisiveness. The way I float through life reminds me of how my eldest daughter Penelope is. It all makes sense now. And as much as I'm not totally surprised by this news, it's still been emotional for me to accept, but it's quite a relief as well.

My diagnosis came about while filming for the documentary in August.

Patrick and I were invited to meet with Sir Simon Baron-Cohen at Cambridge University. He's a professor who studies everything, but autism and the mind is his passion and what he's exploring in-depth. He's the director of the University's Autism Centre and he's been doing lots of research and looking at the genetic side of the condition.

Simon has a real positive outlook on autism and thinks that those who have the condition are amazing, quite rightly so. He was even knighted earlier this year for his services to autism, so it was great to have him in the documentary, but to meet him myself was incredible.

During filming, and to find out if there really is a genetic link with autism, which Simon strongly believes there is, Patrick and I filled out what's called an AQ questionnaire. It tests for symptoms of autism and is recognised globally.

While lots of people might carry a few traits, to actually be classed as autistic you're required to score a high number, and I did. The scale goes from zero to 50 and the average neurotypical person would score up to 15.

While my husband was bang-on average, mine was 36, which is high. I was told this information by Patrick, who went to see Simon before I did.

Chameleon

My husband warned me there was a risk I could be diagnosed as autistic because of the results of the assessment.

Those two weeks between finding out I'd scored high on the test and my official diagnosis from Simon were a turbulent whirlwind of upset and trying to process the idea I could be autistic.

When I eventually went to meet Sir Simon at Cambridge, he carried out a full adult assessment. He quickly put me out of my misery and confirmed I'm autistic. And not just mildly – I'm quite high up the spectrum.

It was a lot to take in and once my appointment was over, I broke down in floods of tears to the documentary director, Lucy. I think it's because the news conjured up a mixture of emotions and while I'm not totally shocked and it's a relief, I'm just really sad for my younger self.

I'm fine now as an adult. Well, I'm not totally fine, there are a lot of things I struggle with every day, but I've learned how to cope with them and I'm quite independent. But when I think back to my childhood, I absolutely needed help, in school especially.

Simon said that I've done really well getting through life without actually knowing I'm autistic and with very little support. We talked about a lot of things and in particular my childhood. It's hard to accept that my condition was never picked up by any of the adults in my life.

"If you were that child now, you would have been diagnosed," he told me.

Sadly, back in the 90s, no one really knew about autism and it wasn't really spoken about, which is another reason I'm keen to spread the word wherever possible. If it means a girl at school struggling with eating or staying focused, like I was, is diagnosed off the back of things I've spoken about, then that's mission accomplished.

But my school was so full with hundreds if not thousands of children, so it's no surprise it got missed. No one even noticed that I didn't eat a meal at lunchtime for years.

Because of my inability to concentrate and my hatred for my school, I left with no GCSEs. I was more than capable of sitting the exams, but I just couldn't be in that exam hall. I remember it so clearly; everyone was on single desks all over the room. I could hear people scribbling their pens on the exam paper and every page turning sounded like a drum banging.

I just sat there and didn't do anything. I didn't lift my pen. What made it even tougher was after a while of staring into space, I got shouted at by the teacher and asked to leave the room. I rushed out in tears and that was it.

Looking back, I would have benefited from someone saying, "What's the matter Christine? Why aren't you doing your exams?" If I could have explained to somebody, "I can't do it in that room. Can you please put me in a separate room on my own?" I would have probably left with really good grades.

It upsets me when I think about things like that, but I

don't think being autistic has held me back in terms of my life plan.

I always wanted to be a mum and a wife, and even if I had achieved straight As, I probably would have followed the path that I'm on now anyway. I know that doesn't sound too ambitious for some people, but that's what I always wanted out of life.

It's just surprising that it's never been picked up by anyone before, because Simon told me that there was no doubt in his mind that I'm autistic.

There's no question for him that there is a genetic link with this condition, and he admitted he kind of knew I was autistic even before we'd even started the official assessment.

The whole meeting was quite conversational. I wasn't being probed or examined, it was more us chatting about how the mind works, things that have happened in life, how I am as a person and the little things that I do every day.

But that grey area after me first doing the test and knowing I'd scored high, before I was officially diagnosed, was a horrendous time. Even though deep down I had an inkling, I'd never had it confirmed from a professor or a doctor before.

It's something my social media followers spotted to be honest and I sometimes think my lovely supporters know me better than anybody.

I don't know what it is I do to give it away, because I think I hide all my little traits quite well, but I've had quite a few DMs saying, "Christine, have you ever been for a test yourself? You come across as quite autistic."

The messages were completely without malice and it's always been lovely words of kindness and concern. It's funny what people notice and I'm sure some of you reading this won't be shocked and always had a sneaky suspicion.

I guess when I suspected I was autistic, I never said anything because I was convinced that without an actual diagnosis people wouldn't believe me. I assumed I came across as quite average. And when it comes to my own children it gives me hope for their future, because I've done it myself without any of the therapies and assistance they've been lucky enough to receive.

It's also confirmed even more so that if they're going to be in relationships, they'll have to meet someone really patient and happy to leave them to it.

I think that's why I've done OK in life, because Patrick was always happy to let me get on with things, while he went off and lived his life. He was more than content for me to stay at home and do nothing.

If I had a partner who wanted me to jet around the world with them and be on their arm at the opening of every envelope, it might sound ideal and like a dream, but it probably wouldn't have worked for me.

I believe it was a good thing I stayed in all those years and eased myself into going out and to small events.

Those little events turned into bigger events and it's only

been the last couple of years where I've gone to parties and red carpets on my own.

It's mad when I think about it, that throughout my twenties, I never had one single night out – not one.

Simon flagged that up when we were chatting.

"Think about it, how many girls in their twenties do you know who never went on a night out, or had girly holidays?" he said to me.

And it's so true. I didn't have a hen party, I didn't have a 16th, an 18th, a 21st, or a 30th. For me, that's normal.

Those are big birthdays that you would normally do something special for, but I reassured everyone, "No, it's fine. I'm quite happy to do nothing." And I was.

I only managed to get through my twenties because I didn't go out. I made every single excuse not to leave the house and socialise. I understand now it's because I'm autistic, and it's much easier to stay in and not have to deal with the real world when you've got autism.

And it's only over the last couple of years since I learnt about the kids' hidden disability that I saw it in myself.

Before I left Cambridge, Simon made sure that it's noted on my medical records that I'm autistic, which is available for my GP – just in case I'm ever in a situation where I might struggle to cope, it's there for my doctors to see. I'm terrible at making decisions so it's good for professionals to know I'm autistic, because you just can't predict what's going to happen to you in the future.

After the appointment I set off on my drive home to Cheshire, and as I made the journey up the M6 I thought about Patrick.

I wasn't sure how he'd react, but when I told him he said he expected it and he'd suspected I was autistic for years – he never thought to tell me!

He just said, "We knew that, didn't we?" Well, I didn't! He was quite blasé about it, but that was his way of trying not to make it into a big deal. He knows better than anyone how to handle me.

Patrick was always conscious that I was a bit different and had my little quirks, but he never understood exactly what it was.

There are times when he gets really frustrated with me, for example when it takes me hours to get ready. Not even when I'm getting fully glammed up, but simple things like picking between two plain T-shirts, and not being able to decide which one to wear.

But he's been really supportive and reassured me, "Anytime I can help you, you know I will do.

"Ask for help if you need it, don't try and do everything yourself."

I think he's worried about everything changing over the next couple of years, because my work life is busier now than ever. I think he's concerned because I've been OK (sort of) and got this far because things have stayed the same or I've been able to adapt slowly.

Chameleon

I find it hard to cope with sudden change.

It was a huge switch in my twenties, going from working and earning loads of money to just staying at home. But once I found myself comfortable hibernating, that was it, I didn't want to go out.

It's about finding the right balance when things are changing for me, to make sure I don't go extreme with it.

When you have autism, you're like a chameleon and constantly transitioning to what you think you're supposed to be. You're always changing yourself to try and blend in.

Like when I became a mum. I just wanted to be a mother that did all the mumsy things, never went out and partied, didn't socialise, looked a bit rubbish and dressed down, because that's how mums are supposed to be. Or so I thought.

But it's been over the last couple of years that I've been mixing it up because I wanted to work.

Now, at 33, with a diagnosis and married with three kids and a new house, I do feel like it's a whole new start.

There's going to be some big changes coming, so I've just got to make sure it's not too much, because I've never had to juggle so much before.

I seem to be on the ball when it comes to the children and their appointments, because I've been really fortunate to be a stay-at-home mum, and I've been able to put all my focus on them. But now that I'm going to be a working mum, I'm really going to have to make sure I look after myself as well. If things get too much, I need to put the brakes on.

But it's important for my children to see me socialising, because I want to lead by example. I've got to show them you can have a life, and I really have tried to make friends. And I can go to events now, whereas in the past, in my twenties especially, I would have completely refused.

I have my own way of doing things when I'm preparing to go out, and I'm at a stage now where a part of me enjoys it. But the majority of the time, I am overthinking everything. I often feel like it's a performance I put on. I try to act like everyone else, and that's typical autism.

It's typical of me, really. That's how I've got through life, by mirroring whoever I'm with.

It's called 'masking' and it's something I've always done. I was very aware of that when I was young.

I remember being in school and thinking that if I copy how other people behave then they might like me. I would always act like whoever I was around at the time. I've done it throughout life, I still do it now and I will carry on doing it. Just because I've been diagnosed as autistic, I can't suddenly change who I am. I was born autistic.

It's still me, but it's learned behaviour. I know that's how to get through life and I don't know any different.

I suppose I'm lucky, as my husband has helped me a lot. Life's been easier because I've been looked after. Not necessarily financially, but he takes care of paperwork and reminds me of appointments. Those are the things I would normally struggle with.

I can imagine for an autistic adult juggling a family and work it could be quite a lot and extremely stressful, but fortunately I've been able to just be a stay-at-home mum for the first few years of my children's lives. I just immersed myself in that and actually found myself really comfortable because I was around my little gang.

I am the best version of me when I'm with my children and that's probably because we're all autistic. The four of us are quite happy to stay in and sometimes not talk to each other. It's when I'm out and about that my autistic mind really goes into overdrive.

For example, if I go into a hotel room, and it makes perfect sense to me now, but I'll rearrange the whole room. If something's not quite straight or if there are pictures on the walls − I'll take them off. If I can, I'll stay in this one hotel. It's in central London and the rooms are the blandest and plainest you've ever seen, but for me it's ideal. I go there and I don't need to start reorganising the room. It's really fascinating and now I understand it's because I'm autistic that I'll go into other hotel rooms and shuffle it around to my taste.

I can sometimes find the carpets or curtains all just too much. If I can't stay in my go-to hotel and I have to stop over somewhere else, like the hotel in Cambridge, I'll be up all night looking at everything.

I'm not slagging off anyone's choices – everyone's got different tastes, and I'm not Mariah Carey saying, "I must walk into a perfect room filled with white lilies." It's just too much pattern is too much for my eyes.

For example, I could be talking to someone and I'll try my best to stay focused on the conversation, but if there is a flowery pair of curtains behind them, I'm going to spend the whole time glaring over their shoulder.

I've learnt as an adult to always be polite and I'd never go into someone's house and say, "Oh my God, your curtains are awful," because they're not, I'm just very easily distracted. Simon explained to me that an autistic person sees the details in everything, which I do.

Even my food struggles I've had throughout my life make sense to me now. It's actually quite a common symptom among women to be how I am with food. It's usually misdiagnosed as something like anorexia, because people assume that women want to look a certain way, but for me it was never that – I never liked how I looked anyway! When my troubles with food began as a child, I never compared myself to celebrities or models. I never even owned a magazine. Trust me when I say the way I looked was the last thing on my mind.

Throughout my life, when people have complimented me, I never believed them. For example, when I was modelling and won pageants, or if I was out with my husband and people would say, "Your wife's stunning."

Or when I get comments on Instagram with people going, "You're beautiful," I never believe it. I just think people are just being nice.

And eating is still a struggle now. I've only tried green food, like broccoli, over the last couple of years. I can eat it, because I know I've got to be healthy, but I never once tried colourful food until my thirties.

It's quite common for autistic people to favour beige food, and that's probably why I didn't see the aversions in the kids, because I just assumed that they're just like me.

Because I was never diagnosed with anything, I never considered their distaste for certain foods a sign of anything. Once they were diagnosed, it did make me think, *oh, I'm a bit like that.*

It never crossed my mind that I needed a diagnosis, I guess I just sort of knew.

So, my autistic traits can range from aversions to patterns, or my issues with food to something really social, like making friends.

I spoke to Simon about my troubles with making friends throughout my life and I realised it's the actual building the friendship part that I find challenging.

I'm OK with small talk and bits of chit-chat with strangers, and I can blag that until the cows come home. But it's when it goes from nice, friendly nattering to someone saying, "We should go for lunch." I immediately put my guard up and think to myself, *God no.*

I'm sure I've met lots of people in my life who have wanted to be my friend and without sounding awful, I don't really want anyone. I'm not great at picking up the phone and I'm not confident with ringing people anyway. I always feel really awkward about it.

I have my close circle, which of course includes Adam and Nelly, and I really feel like I can be myself around them. And having them is more than enough for me when it comes to companionship. I'd rather have two great friends, than loads I wouldn't be able to keep up with anyway.

Nelly won't be shocked when I tell her about my diagnosis, and I feel like deep down she already knows. I've spent more time with her than anyone, but I don't even see her that much. We meet up a couple of times a year at most, and she knows that's enough for me.

I've been on weekends away with Nelly and Adam, and they're both used to my funny little ways.

Like when we stop at a service station and I'm looking at grapes for half an hour and it's a battle in my mind.

"I don't know which grapes to get," I'd say. "Those ones are too round, but these ones are too oval."

They'll just go, "Christine, you're having them." They know if they don't intervene, I'll stand there all day overthinking.

If we're going out, they'll know I'll drag time on for as long as possible – I don't even know why I do that. It's just a constant conversation in my head saying, *do I want to go out?*

And it's not just friendships I struggle to create, but I find it hard to interact with anyone I don't know.

My husband has been asking me to sort out these interior designers for ages, but I just don't want to ring them.

It's funny, because I've been aware of my little quirks for years and even at school, I was incredibly conscious I was different.

I'm OK with it, it's just that other people might find it odd.

It's been difficult for me to understand that others don't do all the things that I do, like preparing a conversation in my head before I meet someone – I just assumed everybody did that! I like talking to myself, that's something I've always done. I thought everyone did that at times, but apparently not.

I've also got slow-processing, which can be a symptom of autism. Some autistic people are really quick and switched on and highly intelligent, and come back with answers instantly, but for me everything takes a while to sink in. It doesn't mean that I'm not intelligent, it's just that I'll be overthinking every little detail.

I constantly have ten things going at once. I'll be shopping in one place, Googling something else, researching autism, and I can't seem to get one thing done.

Even choosing an outfit. I'll stand there looking at my clothes for half an hour.

It's caused so many arguments between Patrick and I,

because I can't make a decision and I can't focus. He'll be talking to me and I'm switched off and thinking about something else. I can't hear him.

If my husband says, "Christine, do you want a sandwich?" I'll spend ages thinking, *has it got butter on? What am I going to have in this sandwich? Shall I cut the crusts off?* If you ask me a question, it might take a couple of seconds to answer, but he says it feels like hours.

It's something I've always been like, and my husband and I laugh about now, which is great.

I'm trying to see my diagnosis as a positive thing – at least I know for definite.

In fact, there are lots of upsides to being autistic, just like there are with the three kiddies.

I'm quite creative and artistic, and I enjoy doing crafts and painting with the children. In fact, art was the only lesson I liked at school.

I'm very organised and a clean freak, so I do struggle with clutter. Since having the children, it's taken me years to get used to everything not being in place where I want it to be. But I have my own little coping mechanisms with everything, and that's how I've probably got to 33 without anyone noticing.

Even when we designed our house, I made sure the kids' rooms had loads of storage so I could close the door on the cupboards and their bedrooms would still look spotless.

As a parent you have to get used to having mess around,

but I absolutely hate it. One of our arguments we're having at the minute is about wallpaper.

Patrick wants to cover our bedroom, the living room and the downstairs toilet in wallpaper, but I just can't bear the thought of it. He's got wallpaper in his office and I can see the seams, so I can't go in there.

So I can be a bit anal when it comes to tidiness, but one of my finest qualities is that I'm very open-minded to people and I think I'm genuinely kind. That's something that's in my children, too.

Not that only autistic people can be kind and caring, but I do think that's a trait and it can be a vulnerability as well – you don't see the bad in people.

I do view myself as quite naïve. For instance, when I've done photoshoots in the past and I've been asked to wear clothes I really didn't like, I'd just wear them with a smile.

Like my children, I'm quite picky with clothes anyway. I like everything plain.

Against my better judgement, I'd always just wear these clothes on the shoot, even though they weren't my style. I think that's because I often misinterpret saying "no" as complaining. I'd never like to appear to be moaning, but then if you don't say anything you're doing yourself a disservice.

I do land myself in some vulnerable situations because of this. It's like when I was a teenager and my peers would say, "Have a couple of shots of vodka, Christine."

"Oh, OK then," I'd reply. But at what age are you going to learn to say "no"?

Recently, I had a text message from Royal Mail saying I needed to collect a parcel.

I always get parcels delivered and it looked legit to me, although now I know it was fraud and I'd just given that con-artist my bloody bank details.

Another example would be when I used to get stopped in Bolton town centre by homeless people selling copies of The Big Issue. It happened quite regularly and I would be that person standing there talking to them for half an hour and giving them £20 before I'd left. It drives my husband insane that I get myself into situations like that.

You do need to be careful. Considering I was raised on a council estate I thought I was really streetwise, but I'm actually not. It's something I need to be more aware of.

There's no doubt that I am a people-pleaser, but I think that's all part of autism. I'm more comfortable when I'm keeping everyone else happy and just going along with things.

And moving on from my diagnosis is going to be a learning curve for all of us. For me, I've always been quite happy, my life's good and I feel quite lucky so I don't want anything to change too much, but I'm aware things might alter slightly this year because of my hectic schedule. I'm just going to have to stop worrying about pleasing everyone.

One of my biggest worries is coming across as a nuisance, because I feel like that anyway. Honestly, I feel like such a hindrance at times, especially with my husband, but with work and events too.

I recently went to an event and my manager must have left me 20 missed calls before I arrived, because I was shockingly late.

I could see my phone flashing and I knew she was ringing me.

I didn't pick up the phone. I wasn't late for any other reason than I was sitting on the bed overthinking.

I felt awful about it, but if I had someone with me that day to go, "Right, are you ready? The car is outside," I would have gone. But because I was on my own in the hotel room, I really had to encourage myself to go. But once I'm out, I do enjoy it.

I know my boundaries and when an event gets too much or too busy, I don't have meltdowns all over the place, I'll just very politely leave.

I'm pushing myself to do things that don't come naturally to me, because I do want to live life and join in. As I've always said, my biggest fear is being stuck indoors again, totally isolated.

It's just in my head, I'm thinking, *I've got nothing to say to people. My outfit isn't right. What if it's too loud, or too busy? What if there's food?* It's that worry that makes me three hours late for everything.

Looking back, so many things that have happened in my life make sense to me.

For example, when I was flying back home from Marrakesh after filming Housewives there.

I couldn't get on the plane and delayed the flight because I was panicking – I realise now I was probably having an autistic meltdown.

I was on the phone to Patrick going, "I don't want to get on the plane, I don't want to get on the plane."

He was going, "You've got to!"

I was at the bottom of the steps to the aircraft and the air hostess said, "Would it make you feel better if you met the pilot?" In hindsight, she was probably just trying to get me on the plane, so they could take off.

And to my surprise, the said pilot was one of the dads from the childrens' school.

"You'll be safe with me," he told me.

"I've got to do the school run on Monday!"

What a coincidence! But even though I felt rather sheepish when I trundled up the aisle to my seat, I made it home.

My head can be all over the place and I sometimes feel like I'm in a film and my head is permanently talking to itself.

And I really struggle with new situations.

Speaking of films, a perfect scenario to try to explain my autism to you is one of the loves of my life, Dirty Dancing.

As you know, that film has always been a passion of mine and I guess because of my autism I obsessed over it.

As a teenager I'd watch it on repeat, over and over again, every single night.

There was just something about it. I really wanted to be one of those women dancing away. And I just couldn't wait to grow up. I always got along better with adults than I did with children, which is probably why I struggled at school.

When I met Patrick at 19, he noticed I had Dirty Dancing pyjamas on and I told him it was my favourite film.

For my 21st, he knew that I didn't want a huge party, and I didn't have friends to invite anyway, so he treated me to a weekend away in London.

It's something most girls would be buzzing about, to be whisked off on a romantic weekend with their partner, but I found it so difficult. In a truly beautiful nightmare situation, I couldn't enjoy it and was all over the place at the time.

I was crying my eyes out, and Patrick and I were arguing the whole weekend. I didn't like the way I looked or what I was wearing.

I'd never been to London and in hindsight I think I was having an autistic meltdown.

Any situation I'm not familiar with gives me major anxiety and fear, because I don't know what to do. It comes across as all wrong and now I understand my children are the same.

But on this weekend, Patrick had arranged to take me

to see the Dirty Dancing theatre show on stage in the West End.

He'll never know this, but I really didn't enjoy it and I've never watched the film since. It just wasn't the same.

When it came to the film, I knew all the dialogue, the whole script from top to bottom, so when we watched this theatre show, right from the opening line it was different. It wasn't my Baby and Johnny.

I really struggled with it, but I hid my disappointment and watched the show with a smile on my face.

The music was nice and the dancing was amazing, but the storyline was slightly different and I haven't been able to watch the film since (sorry, Patrick!).

That's quite typical autistic behaviour. If somebody's obsessed with something and then it's different for whatever reason, then that's it, over.

Something else happened recently which kind of explains how the autistic mind works.

I was driving down to London for work and I made a quick pit stop at the services.

I queued up in Costa and in front of me there was a woman I recognised as autistic, and she had a sunflower lanyard on.

These lanyards are great as they alert other people to the fact that the person wearing one has a hidden disability. But I spotted the autism in her anyway, because of her mannerisms.

She'd ordered this fancy Frostino and she kept insisting to the baristas, "I don't want any milk." She must have said it ten times.

When she went to the pick-up point to collect her drink, I saw her grab the coffee and stare at it intensely.

"This isn't the same, this isn't the same," she said, clearly stressed.

The staff, agitated, replied, "Alright, calm down lady, we'll get you something."

They were probably thinking she was being really rude, but I know for her, in her head, wherever she usually gets her Frostino from, it'll be made in a particular way which is perfect for her.

But when she goes to another Costa and it looks slightly different, for her it was like, *I can't have it. It's not what I ordered and it's not supposed to look like that!*

The staff were really pissed off with her and she was practically marched out of the shop.

It was interpreted wrong, because she's not calmly explaining that it wasn't right for her and she appeared to be quite demanding, so obviously the staff didn't spot the lanyard or understand it and saw her as being a difficult customer.

I did explain to them afterwards, although it probably wasn't my place to do so. But I thought, if in future they can look out for one of those lanyards they might know the customer isn't trying to be difficult, they're just struggling.

So, I wouldn't be surprised if she never goes back to Costa again – just like I won't watch Dirty Dancing ever again.

For me though, the dots have really joined up. And if anything, I feel like it'll be a positive step for me to educate others about autism and perhaps change people's perceptions about what autism can really be like.

I'm hoping my diagnosis will do a lot of good and any women reading this who are unsure about themselves, it might be inspiring to them.

I never thought in a million years I'd ever be considered as an inspiration to anyone, but it's a story that people might relate to.

I'm married with children and I'm working, which are things a lot of people might question whether an autistic person can do. But I'm living proof that, although it's not easy, with a bit of grit, resilience and a supportive family you can achieve anything.

21

Over To You

Having had some time to digest my diagnosis, there are a few things I can take from it.

As well as it being a huge relief, and I understand myself better than ever, I'm certain this can benefit my children, too.

As you're aware, we haven't told them yet that they're autistic. But now it's been confirmed that I am, the fact that they're like Mummy can only make it easier when we do speak to them about it.

I see it as a positive thing, and I would have felt reassured if I was told as a child that other people are like me, too.

It doesn't need to be a bombshell revelation, just a conversation we need to have with the kids.

It's difficult to know when is the right time to discuss

it with them. We talk about their autism openly in front of them, but they've never asked why they go to all these appointments and other children don't, because I think they just assume everyone does.

I believe having this diagnosis is going to help soften it a little bit and I can explain to them, "Mummy's a bit like that and it's OK."

And it shows them that I'm with Daddy, I'm a parent and I have a job. Getting married and starting a family are all things that are totally doable for an autistic person.

They will know that nothing was ever written off and I always believed they would be capable anyway.

Whatever job, career or education path they choose to follow, I'm there to fully support them and I believe they will live some kind of independent life.

My husband and I have met so many autistic adults and young adults while we've been filming the documentary, and the majority of them are striving to have an independent life. They want to go to work and live on their own. They know they need bits of support, but they're OK with it and I think that's great.

When it comes to my own diagnosis, I'm grateful that I found my own little coping mechanisms and I haven't had to deal with the stresses of everyday life. That's thanks to my husband helping me. But it's not one size fits all.

Autism, as I've always explained, comes in all different shapes and sizes and there is a spectrum.

Not all people with autism are like me, and I'm not like others with autism.

When you've met one person with autism, you've met one.

For example, my three children have all got one diagnosis, but they are completely different children, with different personalities and symptoms.

Make no mistake, I relate to them an awful lot and I do believe more than ever a genetic link does exist. It makes even more sense to me now. But we must understand people are different anyway, with or without autism.

And in true Christine style, since receiving my diagnosis, I've been overthinking.

I really worry about changing myself, because I don't want to.

I think I'm OK, but I've lived a life that's very suitable for an autistic person. Everything's been a slow-burner – Patrick's career, our relationship – which is great for me, because I would have struggled to cope with a sudden big change. My life has been very suitable for me and for my children.

I am aware my behaviour isn't 'normal'. I understand that and a lot of what I do is put on. More so when I'm out and about and at events, I'd say it's a performance. But then doesn't everyone have lots of different sides to them, and act in a different way around certain people? It's something to think about.

Another concern is people treating me differently because of this.

I don't want those around me to constantly be like, "Let's make sure Christine is OK."

I really want to avoid that, but I know that probably will start happening. I guess those close to me need to understand I've got through life this far and I can do it, I just have my own little ways of getting by.

Overall, my diagnosis is a positive thing and a big relief, but it's just the devastation for myself as a child.

I'm heartbroken for that Christine. But that's in the past and I've got to look forward to the future and try to take every opportunity, without pushing myself too far.

I really want to just enjoy life and show my children anything is possible and nothing should hold you back – especially your own mind.

I've heard of far too many people who don't like having the autistic label, when actually there's nothing wrong with it. Nothing at all.

It shouldn't put anyone off being your friend or wanting to have a relationship with you. And the more open people are about being autistic, the more we can change the stigma.

And hopefully it will open people's eyes to see that actually, autistic people can present themselves as quite ordinary. It's all about how you think.

You can't see how I think, which is the most autistic part of me. I understand people will struggle to identify it in me, but that's a great thing because it highlights that autism can be difficult to spot.

I'm really excited for when the kiddies are teenagers, to really speak to them about it all.

I want them to really advocate it the way I have done, and I think they will. I think they're going to blow us away with their achievements and keep surprising us like they already do.

There's no rush in life, though, and I'll remind them of that. I've only just started to get into work, and that's OK.

I want to teach my children to find their feet, grow and develop.

It's funny because they're not aware of how much of an impact they're already making. They don't understand what Mummy and Daddy's jobs are and can't yet comprehend what a 'celebrity' is.

I've heard other children say to them at school, "Your daddy works on Top Gear," and people go, "Oh, I watched your mummy on television yesterday." But the kids just don't know any different. They just think everyone's mums and dads do that. I actually think they think Daddy just drives cars – Patrick is basically a glorified chauffeur. But I love that about them.

And one of the other positives I can take from my diagnosis is that it's helped me with my worries for my children that I confided in you about.

It's not that they've totally gone, but I do think it's put

my mind at rest a bit when it comes to their future. They can be quite capable because I am.

For example, my daughter Penelope – I see so much of myself in her. If she meets the right person, like I did, someone who can accept her for who she is and let her be her quiet little self – and if she wants to go to her room for four hours, let her do it – then she'll be just fine.

This beautiful nightmare has been a real journey for me, and it's ongoing. If I was to write another book from now, where my career's just beginning, it would be a completely different tale. I do feel my life is just starting, in so many ways. Work is really kicking off this year and it does feel like a whole new me.

I've always overthought and questioned everything about myself. I've had an eating disorder, been sexually abused, raped, my mum had depression, my dad is a heroin addict and was never around, and we grew up with absolutely nothing. I also struggled to get pregnant and my marriage has been difficult at times. And then my mum got cancer.

But there's nothing else that can happen that will knock me back down, so I'm just trying to enjoy the second part of my life as best I can.

When you think things can't get any worse, some people will focus on the worst, but you can't live in the past.

Before now, I constantly questioned who I am, what I'm doing and what my purpose is. But now everything has just fallen into place.

My calling was always to be a mum – but a mum of three autistic children, and to grow a following.

I'm still building my platform and working on it, and I'm using it to raise awareness for autism. And that's what I want to do. At this time in life, I just feel more comfortable with myself and standing up for what I believe in.

When it comes to looking ahead to the future, for me the focus is always going to be on my kids – making sure they're thriving in school, getting Felicity settled in primary school and praying for no more lockdowns.

I want my marriage to carry on going strong, and for us to continue supporting each other and juggling the way we do. Career-wise I want to keep working. I don't know where or what I see myself doing.

There's no end goal, but I just want to be successful. I don't ever want to be someone who goes to the opening of an envelope, because I could spend that time with my children. I only want to get involved in projects that are going to make a difference, like charity work, or if I'm going to enjoy it. I love having a laugh and if there's something I think I'll really enjoy, then I'll do it.

More than anything, I'm so grateful for the life I have. Not because I live in a fancy house, but because I live in a house with enough bedrooms for my children and we're not fighting over having the electricity on.

The children have televisions, we've got a car that gets us from A to B and I'm really grateful I'm not where I was. I'm not on the council estate where I grew up and I'm grateful my children have got more in life. And I'm really pleased they are in a school where they're not just a number, they're understood and looked after. But most importantly, I'm so thankful that I understand them.

And the other positive from this is that it's made me even more determined to raise awareness, if that's even possible.

According to the National Autistic Society, one in a hundred people are diagnosed as autistic, but in reality, there's probably a lot more out there who have gone undiagnosed.

It's not recognised or understood enough and there's people living every day without support, like I was as an adolescent.

There are people who get diagnosed in adulthood, who have always been told they're awkward, rude, single-minded, fussy, odd or different.

There are people who will have been called all kinds of things, when actually they're just autistic. But it's something we are trying to do something about.

The best thing I've ever done and will ever do in my whole life is raise awareness for autism. The kids' diagnoses have changed my life in such a good way, because it's made me stand up, use my voice, speak out and really try to help. I really do want to make a difference.

I want autistic children and adults to live in a world that understands them. Everything I do, every penny I raise, any time I speak about it, any interview I do, it's for my kids and it's all thanks to them. They're changing the world without even knowing it.

Hopefully when they're older, they'll stand up, be proud and talk about it as well. For now, I can only speak from a parent's point of view. But I just think they're incredible.

When it comes to the stigma, there was a quote on Instagram that really struck a chord with me.

"I promise to teach my babies to love your babies," it read.

It was in response to the horrific racial abuse some of the England players received after the Euros final against Italy in the summer and how we can tackle racism in our society. It made me think about children with disabilities and autism.

I teach my children how to communicate with others, but I don't think everyone does. Things like how to be more patient with additional needs, and to not point if you see someone acting out.

If some parents aren't teaching it, shouldn't there be mandatory education about this subject?

It's sad that it's something we even have to consider, but I do feel like we've lost our path a bit and this next generation is going to have a lot to deal with.

So, if you see someone jumping up and down and flapping their hands really excitedly, don't stare. Just think to yourself, *he's probably autistic.*

If it's more recognised and people understand it then they'll know what to do, such as give them space when they need it.

If a child's having a meltdown, don't automatically go, "Oh, what awful parents, they can't control them."

That child's probably dealing with sensory overload, and that's not their fault.

It's part of who they are and how they deal and cope with things.

The reason I push my social media, the reason I work, everything, is because if my profile goes up, I can talk more about autism, reach a bigger audience and hopefully make a difference for my children.

The world has to do their bit too and hold their hands up and say, "We're not doing enough for disabled people. We're not treating them equally." I do think it's going to take a huge movement, and sadly people won't want to admit to the failings there have been so far.

Having said that, the government is taking great steps. It's pledging to make the diagnosis time faster and investing a staggering £75million into its plan. It's aiming to tackle the inequalities and barriers that autistic people face and sort out better access to health and social care. It will also support education, to help with the needs of autistic people. And the strategy includes plans to support those getting into employment, and to develop the public's understanding of the condition.

Things are changing, and I'm excited for our children's future. In ten years' time the twins will be 18, which is scary. I think, wow, look at how much has already happened in the last couple of years, and how things have progressed.

Four years ago, when we revealed that our children are autistic, it was a massive story and we weren't expecting such a big response.

That just goes to show that even four years ago it was quite a big deal for people to hear that we had autistic children, and it came as a massive shock. But while there has been some great progress made when it comes to autistic awareness, we've still got a long way to go. Hopefully, one day it will be completely accepted and just one of those things.

So, what I ask from you, my loyal followers, readers, fans and supporters, is if you see someone in Costa appearing to be rude, if you see a child having a huge meltdown in a supermarket, or if you see someone parked in a disabled space who looks physically abled, please, stop and think and look out for the lanyards.

Autism is a hidden disability for exactly that reason – it's hidden! Let's change the stigma together.